In My Lifetime

Solicitude

John T. Eber Sr.

MANAGING EDITOR

A publication of

Eber & Wein Publishing

Pennsylvania

Library of Congress
Cataloging in Publication Data

ISBN 978-1-60880-232-6

Proudly manufactured in the United States of America by

Eber & Wein Publishing

Pennsylvania

A Note from the Editor...

We are elated to welcome our published poets and appreciators of art to this beautiful collection of contemporary literary talent. Within these bound pages, we have rendered eclectic portrayals of life in well-crafted verse fit for interpretation, comprehension, identification and, above all, celebration. Historically throughout all cultures, poetry has been an art form of vindication, nourishment, imagination and communication. It has also been aesthetically satisfying—both writing and reading poems are undeniably pleasurable acts. While poetry has sustained its cultural significance and delectable allure, poetic exhibition has unfortunately been marginalized in more recent times. Nowadays, outside of creative writing courses and small coffee house or bookstore readings, poems are most notably recited at presidential inaugurations, funerals and weddings. Poets are not socially emboldened to share their work as they once were, and praise for the craft and condition of the poet is not as pronounced as it once was. Yet, our connection to poems and thus their significance is far more expansive than particular, rare instances in which they are showcased; furthermore, the amount of poets actively creating skillful composition is excitedly astounding. Thus, we are passionately devoted to presenting all kinds of poets writing all sorts of poetry, and we are inspired to continue the poetic tradition of transmitting cultural and personal perspectives in hopes of recording and reaching greater understanding.

Poetry's emotional and existential impact on readers rivals any other form of writing; it is richly concentrated, rigorously concise, and ripe with potent imagery capable of terrifying, exciting, distressing, redeeming, amusing and calming readers. In poetry, we find reflections of ourselves—fragments of our experiences and understandings. As William Carlos Williams expresses in "Asphodel, That Greeny Flower," "My heart rouses/ thinking to bring you news/ of something/ that concerns you/ and concerns many men..." This is why it is so important to not only write poetry, but read the works of other poets. Doing so not only enriches our understanding of ourselves, it also expands our consciousness of others and develops in us sympathy and appreciation for those whose particular circumstances may differ from our own life experience. Therefore, poetry is culturally righteous and in every sense of the word sublime, as it teaches us invaluable lessons by revealing the commonality among us all in relation to our human condition. For this transcendence alone, poetry is priceless.

Take this opportunity to rejoice at your impressive accomplishments and read the array of unique creations featured within these pages; keep in mind how blessed we are to be moved to write, how grateful we should be to behold the art of others, and how wise we are to know the essential value in poetic expression. Sigmund Freud, the father of psychoanalysis and an avid enthusiast of poetry and poets, once said, "Everywhere I go, I find that a poet has been there before me." As you delve into this compilation, we encourage you to reminisce on where you've been—perhaps out of where you have gotten—and where your life has yet to take you.

Rachel Rogers
Editor

R.I.P. Grams

It came to me by chance
I didn't have a clue
For no reason, it came into my possession
It came from Grams
Whom I barely knew
I keep it close and hidden
That way people's nasty, dirty words
Don't tarnish the few
Memories of her
Looking back
I'm left to wonder
Did she know
Know she wasn't going to see me again
And that she wanted me to remember?
Grandma Susan died the day after she graced me with the ring
Looking back on that time
I feel empty, lost, cold
And I spiral deeper into the black
It's not a picture
But it holds a photo
It holds memories
She is part of it
You may have taken your last breath on this earth
But you're still here
And Grandma Susan, I will never forget. . .

Dana Lee Parsons
Nunica, MI

The Line

Gave up my name,
Gave him my life;
I love this man,
I am his wife.
While I played house,
My role was "mother."
My husband,
He took a lover.
What about our vows?
What about trust?
He gave it up,
He gave into lust.
My pillow wet with tears,
So many wasted years.
Time to leave this life behind—
He has crossed the line.

Andi-Maria London
Waxhaw, NC

God's Rainbow

After the rain has fallen from the sky,
flames of the rainbow light the imagination of God and I.

Red images color my life of splendor,
red flames of His rainbow surround me so tender.

Purple flames soar the passage of what I will find—
I run to purple shade of the rainbow of my mind.

Burning green rapture has found the rain of night and day;
green flames amaze the wonder of His rainbow today.

Yellow flames throw embers of the sun in the land of the rainbow:
sun of day together with the midnight sun dance all aglow.

Orange arch of the rainbow is bliss of dawn and twilight,
orange flames of rhapsody adorns my sight.

Blue flames burst among the sun, moon and stars upon the bay;
haze of blue charms the summit of the rainbow faraway.

Passion of indigo fascinates the aura of tomorrow. . .
indigo flames chase the rainbow's shadow.

Black flames are the keepsake of a thousand raindrops—
this is the key that unlocks a thousand teardrops.

After the rain has fallen by the window,
I have the flaming promise of God's rainbow.

Clara L. Higgins
Broken Bow, OK

To My Love

I awake from troubled sleep—black clouds
make me wonder if I am even sane
You reach out and draw me near
and sunshine floods my being again.

I search the crowded room
looking for your familiar face
then I see your sudden smile
My world is completely in place

If I should take my long journey
before you get your call from on high
don't mourn for me, my darling
only hold my hand 'til I say, "goodbye"

Mable Fowler
Sedalia, MO

The Price of Freedom

Oh, Freedom
What is your price?
You are visibly represented
witnessing a soldier
holding a bundle of flags,
placing one beside a gravestone.
Your price has a ripple,
in many untold, unseen places.
You left the battlefields
secured in sacrifice
by many men and women.
The price of freedom
continued in peace
in the minds and lives
of those soldiers.
Enemies invaded in places
of church, job, and home.
Oh, Freedom, your price
was costly in the home.
Broken bodies will be repaired—
why not broken minds
that cause the broken homes?
Freedom will always be fought
for the oppressed of nations.
At home, there is a new soldier
drafted in love into service.
Oh, Freedom, may your price
knock on Heaven's door,
so comfort may rain down on all.

Judith E. Tarbox
Charlotte, NC

As a veteran of the United States Navy (1/19/73–10/31/75) and a member of the American Legion, I participated in the biannual changing of the flags on veterans' graves. My husband, also a veteran, was the inspiration for my poem. He was changing flags, creating a magnificent sight. Several days later, these words flowed out.

Aw, Nuts!

Hi, I'm Gus!
I'm going off to the vet today.
We're riding in the car;
I've been there before, I know the way,
It isn't very far.
It's really fun to go for a ride and I really like the vet.
I don't know why I'm going, they haven't told me yet.
I don't think I'm sick, I'm feeling okay...
Maybe it's shots I'm getting today.
Up on the table, checking my rear,
I've been passing some gas—maybe that's why I'm here?
Watch it there, Doc, you're getting too low...
You can look, you can feel, but they're not there for show.
Here comes the shot. Boy, it's a doozy;
I've had these before, but I never got woozy.

I really was out! I'm just coming to...
I'm beginning to wonder: just what did they do?
I think they took something that I wanted kept;
I'm certain they took it some time while I slept.
They never asked me—no ifs, ands, or buts.
They did it. They stole them. Gosh darn it! Aw, *nuts!*

Russ Penne
Kalispell, MT

Mother Teresa

Ten-finger magnet,
steel-crane back
bent irreversibly,
picking up humanity
encrusted with jewels
of dirt and sores. . .

Eyes weeping love:
hearing silent cries,
smelling sacred decay.
Lips smiling sadness,
arms holding beloveds. .. .

Hands painting
masterpieces of farewell
to canvas-covered corpses. . .

Patricia Skydancer
Albuquerque, NM

During my lifetime, I have been an artist: painting, sculpting, writing biographies, and poetry. "Mother Teresa" is a "word painting" of the humble magnificence and spiritual purity of Mother Teresa. I pray the poem captures and expresses the essence of her "being." My deceased daughter, Diane Katrina Demchuk, encouraged and inspired me.

Summer

Surrounded by the wet wilderness of a sweltering Southern summer,
listen to the whisper-hum of mosquitoes racing to suck.
Weather—hot, humid, heat, occasionally cut by scant gulf breezes.
Sweat pours as you discover delicious forests of fragrant green gardens. . .
Treetop moss mansions fill the sky
and darken the ground for your only refuge.
Children kept busy by fishin' holes and elusive fireflies,
Adults escape—no longer immune to, or enthralled by, the season.
I dream of the mercury drop that will bring out autumn's palette.

William Jackson
League City, TX

Ghetto Hope

Lost, little angel in the devil's playground
Looking to the sky, hoping someone's looking down
Holding onto her doll, 'cause that's the only thing that cares
Hard to see her beauty when it's covered by despair
Walking the concrete jungle and all that she sees
Is the heel and makeup-wearing reflections of what she's meant to be?
Lost, little angel, I know you can spread your wings
With God as your guide, I know you can find your dreams

Jacory Reynolds
Vicksburg, MS

Thinking of You, My Departed

I had a dream of you and saw your ghost,
who told me to open your closet and go through a particular box.
The first thing I saw was a photo of your hamster that died;
It used to sit on your shoulder when you read the paper,
It would sh*t in your hand, a really true friend.
I miss your smell, and the way you made tea,
and how you always found a way to make fun of me.
I'll tell you what ghost,
let's make a deal—because I'm not sure if I'm crazy,
or if seeing you is real.
If I die any time soon, let's go to Las Vegas and sing to the moon.
Let's ride the clouds to Los Angeles and laugh at the stars,
let's steal celebrities' cats and fart in their cars.
I have to admit, it's nice and quiet
now that you're no longer alive.
There's no one who snaps at me or makes me feel sad;
I don't really feel lonely, so I'm really glad.
The fights we'd have over nothing are done,
and the funny thing is, I know I always won.
So continue to haunt me, now that you know the truth—
and when I die, I'll see you
and you can kick me through the roof.
But until that day, really, leave me alone,
Because I'm trying to move on
And find peace in this home.
Do what you will, say what you'll say;
And for your memory I'll continue to pray.
But if your ghost crosses me and prevents me from living my life—
I'll never regret killing you
with that kitchen knife.

Lara Martine Lenhoff
Plano, TX

Breaking Bonds

You hang onto the branch,
Surrounded by your closest friends.
You all look so much alike,

from your shape, to your size,
to the color and your imperfections.
The spitting image of the leaves right beside you.

Nestled closely together, like sardines in a can.
Your thoughts pulse through your veins, as you hang on
by a little string that keeps you dangling.

A bond keeping you from reaching the ground.
Although you look similar to your peers,
You are unique, and can change.

In the spring,
you are a soft, newly born green;
Summer makes you tan and grow.

The fall lets you stand out most of all,
Glowing as bright as the colors of the sun...
But then, there is winter.

A cool, crisp, biting force,
Coming sneakily as a cat.
Breaking your bond—

Making you fall to the ground, alone and helpless.

Makayla Tuomi
Clarkston, MI

Everyday People

They smile, they cry, they pass us by
they look as though they are thinking
Without a doubt, they've figured out
we can't solve problems by drinking

Everyday life is changing fast
and people express different moods
If there was a time, let it be now
that we come together and not brood

I know not to ask, but to demand
that everyday people help us help
those who cannot prosper in life
and not keep world knowledge to yourself

Everyday people are not just they
who have access to every floor
but those who we forget about
ones we push behind closed doors

One question to those who don't show a care
Why not help those with whom the world we share?

Melody Sullivan
Helena, AR

Black and White

You try to make it up to me
But too many bridges have been burned
It's too hard for you to see
The page has already been turned

Our differences are too great to alphabetize
Our similarities, too sparse to number
But it's too late to apologize
To me, you've become lumber

You try to make me explain
But obviously, you can't see
Our friendship is detained
We are too different to be

But maybe there is hope for our alliance
Maybe we just need time
Your actions turned into defiance
A mountain that I couldn't climb

Tomorrow is a new day
I will find a new buddy
We have gone our separate ways
Those last few days were just cruddy

I see you walking on the street
I see you with your friends
I wish I could take back all those things I said
But our friendship must come to an end

Baylea Sophia Bills
Coweta, OK

Cry for the Children

A child is more precious than any gold
They are the world, truth be told

So why must we cry for the children?
I'll give you a hint:
Each and every child was Heaven-sent!

We cry for the children
And no matter how many times tears are shed
We'll never answer the question
Why our children are dead

When they die for reasons untold
The world becomes dark and very cold
The gifts that are our children, alas, won't grow old

We cry for our children because we must
We cry for the children who trusted us

Charles Cobb
Kittrell, NC

Contagious Hate

Many have gazed upon this shattered heart,
This misery is tearing him apart.
She should have left well enough alone. . .
No smiles for a love from the unknown.
Happiness escapes his painful thoughts;
She twisted him so strenuously taut.
Empty holes behind her empty eyes,
Empty thoughts filled under falling skies.
Sharp, venomous fangs of despair—
A disease, no one seems to care.
Every "I love you" was meaningless and ever so
Fatal, a dagger twisted deep inside his torso.
Will a day ever come
When deception meets done?
A hole remains where his heart once was;
Her heartless evil was just because.
Hate has consumed his soul,
Hate has taken its toll.
He is dead on the inside.
Hate fills all who have tried.
He spreads his emptiness. . .
No one will remain blessed.

Jason Robert Young
Troy, MI

A Princess Proud and True

I am a princess
I am brave and strong
Kids that have cancer, I will help
Volleyball and soccer is what I want to do
Kids that get bullied, I will help
I may get bullied, but that's okay
Advice from my mom helps
She tells me to control my reaction to other people's actions
I am a princess
I am brave and strong
Proud and true
I am a princess
And saving the world is what I will do

Airiyannah Yanyla Irie Washington
Kansas City, MO

Brother

Brother, O brother, where art thou brother?
Did you die, were you hurt?
Brother, O brother, where have you gone?
We were once such good friends, and now
We are nothing but mere strangers passing in the street.
Brother, O brother, you are here—but not here—
You are gone, dear brother of mine.

Amanda Carpino
Churchville, NY

Clowns of Self

Always a smile
  never a frown:
these are the expected ways
  of a clown.
Inner emotions never
  outwardly known,
tears and fears never
  outwardly shown.
These are the clowns of self.
  Eyes always bright,
    facing the sun,
but when the lights go out. . .
  my colors, they run.
These too, are the
  clowns of myself.

Tamra Denise Weaver
Andrews, TX

My Dog Ace

No one will ever take your place.
When I close my eyes, I still see your face.
You were always by my side,
except for when you went outside.
At only four years old, you died;
I was so unhappy I cried and cried.
Your head was hit by an awful blow—
you tried to fight it, but you still had to go.
But the joy you gave me I won't forget...
thoughts of you stay with me yet.
The silly grin you made me laugh,
along with the wiggle you had in back.
Your fierce growl and bark made people stay back,
but I knew you were just like a pussy cat.
I remember how you flipped a biscuit off your nose
and caught it when I said,
and the way you always hogged the bed.
I loved you Ace and my tears will always be,
Because you aren't here beside me.
Now your in heaven where good dogs go;
I will be with you again someday, I know.
Then you can make me laugh again,
Only God knows how much I miss you, my friend.
So while you rest with no pain, in peace,
till I see you again, my tears won't cease.

Toni Norris
Ashland, OH

To Dream, Or Not to Dream?

To dream, or not to dream? This is what I've been questioning.
Whether 'tis right for my mind to ponder
The very thing that causes my heart to fly,
Or to become face-to-face with what's before me,
And by dreaming a way out? To see, to sour;
In hopes of more; and to dream a dream that would end
Life's misery and a thousand generations to follow
And yet so much more. 'Tis a beautiful consuming
Thought to be wish'd upon: To see, to sour,
To dream: in chances of viewing more. .a.future
Beyond what tomorrow's morrow brings.
For then, time as we once knew it
Would only leave us with the memories.
What we think is the end appears to be an everlasting beginning.
For then we would only once know of struggles,
Those struggles once made life drag us by.
Then again, dreaming makes us escape from the present,
Leaving us face-to -face with what's before us.
Becoming absent to reality
Can become a trap—an exit for a while,
Letting us believe that our "world" is better
Than the real one that we shortly pass by.
Is it right for a man to question the very thing
That drives him insane?
Again, I begin the never-ending question: What is right,
What is wrong? To dream, or not to dream?
Unanswered silence is medicine that kills—
My mind is left split in two.

Jennifersara Alpert
Voorhees, NJ

Carry Me Away

Once upon a time, long ago,
In a dream, I thought of you.
Walking alongside me, I looked upon you—
Into your crystal eyes and into your spirit.
My spirit, so trapped; you caught me
And carried me away, so far away.
Many things clear, others just a haze.
I see light: very bright, but so far away.
I see rocks, boulders, and the light...so bright.
The light pulls me forth, while the rocks hold me back.
Trapped in spirit, tired soul,
Lift me up while held down tight.
Then a rainbow and a bird up above so high. . .
A call for me, blinding me, my senses keen,
Well-aware. Self-aware.
A loaded volcano, ash all around,
Many layers surrounding me, covering me, sheltering me.
A storm of sorts, but somehow refreshed;
The wind blows past as fresh as the sea,
The smell of rain overtaking me.
Soon, I'm soaked—as clean as can be,
Free of dust, dirt and debris.

Heather M. Kind
Blackfalds, AB

Free to Be

Walked along a meadow lane
while Joy strolled by my side.
We held hands, forgetting pain,
and laughed until we cried.

We kissed farewell and waved adieu
without grasping to hold on.
This became a treasure true
in Eternity's near dawn.

Trudged along a forest trail
with Sorrow arm in arm.
Tried to smile, to no avail,
then smelled sweet Sorrow's charm.

Her eyes were deep as we hugged goodbye;
I touched her flush-red cheek.
My spirits lifted, oh, so high,
touching Heaven in my being meek.

Emil P. Myskowski
Lake Ridge, VA

Over recent decades, a habit of daily prayer-journaling has taken root. This practice has proven illuminating to the spiritual journey. Honesty has been the guiding principle in writing entries, no matter how painful or befuddled they may be. Out of the jumble of experiences and observations, every once in a while, a poem that expresses a snapshot of life emerges. Having retired from industry and government careers in aerospace reconnaissance satellite systems and from thirty years of pastoral ministry as a Catholic Permanent Deacon, the grandfather time has come to harvest this poetry to share.

In January

Finally, a day filled with the light, void of heavy
I drove to the sea
walked out by myself
to gaze at the silver, grey and salmon sky at twilight
And I dug for a familiar tone
and under that
to set the backdrop, as the sky was falling apart and breaking into night
But I found nothing
no longing
no sadness
no missing
no love
Just me
in the not hot
not cold weather
not particularly crowded sidewalk
Now, was I alone
I realized, somewhere
in one of the days past
that I had released the grip from my fingers
and let go of all that no longer was holding on
And it felt good
to disappear with the sun
and lighten up with the darkness illuminating the moon

Sunny Rey
San Diego, CA

Can You Say What I Mean?

Now I think
Now I say
The word
But it does not sound the same.

Why does my mouth
not make
the sound I want
why can I not say what I mean?

Is it that I do not try
Is it that I do not mean it
Is it that I care too much?
I wish I knew.

If I try harder
If I say more
If I look at you
Will you understand?

Stephen D. Kearney
Whitefish Bay, WI

When I Am

When I am alone, you are with me
When I am in sick, you heal my afflictions
When I am in life's storms, you bring me peace
When I have given up, you tell me to try again
When I am heartbroken, you pick up the pieces
When I am selfish, you are selfless
When I forget who I am, you remind me
When I feel unloved, you wrap your arms around me
When I am weak, you make me strong
When I am in darkness, you show me the light
When I make mistakes, you help me fix them
When I disappoint, you always take me back
When I am hurt, you love me
When I push you away, you pull me back in
When I am tired, you give me rest
When I mess up again, you take me back again
When I am blind, you open my eyes so I can see
When I am hungry, you give me food
Without you, I am nothing—without me, you are still everything

Kara Rachel Eads
Bedford, IN

Words

Coming, dripping, painting:
pictures streak from coursing keys.
Letter by structural letter,
letter by beautiful letter,
flowing rivers from my unworthy mouth.

Spilling, gathering, forming—
images of mountains I will never see,
people who will never grace me with their beautiful faces,
crowding my skull, begging to be spat upon the page.

Scratching, screaming, begging
for a chance to be encased in glorious words,
petrified in stale ink, immortalized in unforgiving letters. . .
bound to paper that will long outlive their wilting, flesh-bound prisons.

The frail mountains will have long crumbled,
while the invincible words live on, eating away at worthy hosts
until the parasite of droning lines has succeeded—
breaking free into spectacular colors upon the unexpecting page.

Painting pictures never seen,
faces never needed.
As the host hand scrawls the sloppy words across the page,
the parasite has transformed from the ugly feeding larvae
into a radiant, delicate poem.

Jessica M. Schampers
Milwaukee, WI

Broken: Not Forever?

In time was created a strong, independent me
My fight—against the stereotype
Influenced and supported to be individually unique
I won't be broken.
Walls I built on high,
But only in my mind's eye
I can be broken.
Life lost around me,
Happiness stolen from me.
Compromises...compromises,
All in the name of love?
Hands can break,
Pain breaks.
Looking at my portrait,
Broken shards of beautiful, blown, colored glass—
Tangible, fragmented memories
Interspersed with shattered pieces
Of the mirror of my once whole self-reflection.
My fingers caress the sharp edges...
A quick captured stare, my eye returns an empty look.
Can it be undone?
Or, in the least, pieced together once more?
I am a daughter, sister, teacher—
A woman who once knew.
Now your wife, your love, your life, by your side.
Only you can bring together what you have broken...won't you?

Rehana Ahmed
Gaithersburg, MD

Mistake

I stand alone
enemies penetrate my guilt
deep within, my soul moans
all I built
shattered and spilt

Who will forgive
a withered being?
One who humbly lives
Branded and steaming
my mind shuns the meaning

Clueless are you
guilty am I
able, I stand anew.
Smothered, I cry
"Why endure and try?"

I care for only one
haunted by another.
An example to shun
legend or other
I journey no farther.

Anika Nicole Blackmore
Bonners Ferry, ID

When Things Go Wrong

When things go wrong, and they sometimes will,
when the road you're traveling seems all uphill,
when the funds are low and the debts are high,
when you want to smile, but you had to cry,
when care is pressing you down a bit,
rest if you must—but just don't quit.

Life is odd, with it's twist and turns,
as each of us will sometimes learn.
But many a failure turns about,
and we can win. .if.we stick it out.
Don't give up, though the pace seems slow;
you may succeed with the very next blow.

Often, the goal is near at hand—
so always work as hard as you can.
If you want the golden crown and the victor's cup,
just hold on and don't give up.
Stick to the fight when you are hardest hit. . .
it's when things go wrong that we must not quit.

Carol Woodham
Dothan, AL

Betrayal

Tell me it wasn't you
Would you turn
Would you betray me
Without concern?
Will we ever come to learn?
Just one more chance
Explain this to me
Your place without
This family tree
Our trust in you in jeopardy
Could it be that you turn your back
This easily
On this thing you call your family?
I don't understand why you would
Or how you could
This isn't the way
I thought it would be
A family with no *Daddy*.

Allie Mitchell
Stephenville, TX

The Night Visitor

We have a night visitor
who waits till all is silent
then begins to nibble away
on what we cannot fathom.

We wondered about the candy
in the bowl on the counter.
Till one day his, or her, "leaving"
we began to encounter.

We first thought it was seeds
that had fallen from our hair. . .
but soon realized those ideas
were all for the air.

Still, we've no trace of
from whence it came. . .
How it got in is
still a puzzle game.

But one day, we will
be able to send. . .
this visitor to its end!

That we did with a raisin and trap. . .
so guess we'll have to take the rap
'cause we can't abide a mouse
of any size in the house!

So we can say, "So long, and goodbye"
with not one tear in either eye!

Betty Jo King
Massillon, OH

Betty Jo King (*continued*)

As a child, we had a regular Christmas "visitor," termed a mouse. It was always checking the out-of-state family gifts. It was a very large "mouse," because the corner holes were huge. I wrote about this "visitor" in a story, called "The Maysel Mouse," named for the community in which we then lived. It is a true but fun story which became the background for "The Night Visitor," written a few years ago. We were awakened one night by a noise in our bedroom wall. The visitor was having a nice time travelling among the boards. We later found out it also liked Hershey's kisses. It was very crafty in getting away for a day or two, but we were also crafty and soon ended its wandering days. Since the death of my hubby, I have had many "lost" days, and writing down my thoughts has been very helpful; it has also presented many learning moments. I thank God for giving me this ability to gather my thoughts. I am almost seventy-seven years old and enjoy writing, singing, woodworking and many other activities with my church, family and friends. God has blessed this family with a wonderful leader, my hubby Bill: father, granddad and family "Mr. Fix-It."

In the Eyes of the Beholder

Have you ever enjoyed a sunset
at the end of a hectic day?
Have you ever caught the smile of a child
during an afternoon of play?
Have you ever breathed the fresh, clean air
after a violent thunderstorm, or
followed the brilliant colors of a rainbow
into a field of tasseled corn?

If these things you haven't experienced,
it is time to take a break
from the troubles and uncertainty;
your happiness is at stake.

There are simple things to make a day
a happy memory in your mind—
from butterflies to dewdrops,
or the touch of someone kind.

Keep any eye out for the little things
that get lost along the way—
They will be there to keep you going,
no matter how hard the day.

Linda Bickos
Unadilla, NY

The Quilting Squares

As I sit here sewing
My mind goes back in time
I wonder about the woman
Whose labor now is mine
The quilting squares, so old, some stained
The fabric aged, antique, yet plain
The dusty box was just left there
In the corner against a chair
I ponder was it a mistake?
Did they realize, but all too late?
In bold letter across the back
Grandmother Cobler penned in black
In scribbled hand on top it read
Have Lewis store this in his shed
My thoughts went back; had they looked inside
Seen the treasure, felt the pride?
Grandma's hands had done it all
Every stitch—so tight, so small
I sit here taking on the task
To finish what is from the past
Warm feelings embrace me, hard to explain
And all I know...is just her name

Pat Rogers
Montell, TX

My brother worked at a private warehouse. Someone moved out and took everything but a box of material and an old chair. He gave the box to me; it was marked "Grandma Cobler's quilting pieces—have Lewis put in storage." When I opened the box, to my surprise, there were twenty finished, hand-sewn quilting squares. Some of my friends who are quilters assured me the material was so old it could not be replaced, and they encouraged me to finish what Grandma Cobler had started. I mentioned all of this to my friend Marty, who said, "Somewhere, Pat, there is a poem in there." Her words stuck in my mind, and one night while riding in the car, this poem came bubbling out of my inner-most being. I turned on the overhead light and grabbed pen and scrap paper. This is my favorite poem to date.

The Monster of Me

I'm standing in the rain
Trying to wash away the pain
Praying that the falling water puts a silence to the flames

So I stand here and pretend
If I lean against the wind
A gust will come and blow away all the darkness from within

Hoping that I will grow cold
Like the ice that's is the snow
As I feel the monster eating, ripping, gripping at my soul

I try and try not to see
I pray and pray it just can't be
But in the end, I must accept that the monster here is me. . .

Nigel Leon Thomas
Miami, FL

The Last Retreat

In the calm
of a mid-morning sun
in mournful silence
rests a lonely
flag-draped casket.
Hushed words are uttered
by a black-cloaked figure
Cut short by a resounding echo
of three-seven round volleys
and an unseen bugler blows
the somber last retreat.

The scene has been repeated
and shall continue to go on,
as long as we do not remember
what befell us in our past.
The young among us now
stand at the ready
to serve, protect and defend—
much as we did then.

In the tearful calm
of setting sun ,
over the mournful, echoing silence
resounds the haunting
refrain of taps:
last retreat.

Jerald H. Lucas
Scottsbluff, NE

A Little Risque...in a Bookish Sort of Way

I'm in love with my Thesaurus,
He's always by my side.
When I'm at a loss for words,
He gladly opens wide.

I adore my Thesaurus.
He whispers in my ear.
I embrace his every page,
With words I long to hear.

I'm passionate for my Thesaurus,
I sleep with him at night;
He waits upon my bedstand,
until the mood is right.

I cherish my Thesaurus;
He please me, it's true.
Without desirous wordage,
what would a writer do?

Linda Niewiadomski
Woodbridge, VA

From My Heart

There once was a boy who was filled with pride and joy
he jumped and played and ran through the house
trying to be as quiet as a mouse
As I looked at him I could see
a man among men
plain as can be

There once was a boy who grew to be
a man among men
how proud I can be
Oh, God, help me, as I can see
this man among men
will soon leave me

This man among men
will soon be wed—as I hope and pray his wife can see
a man among men
as their son will be

A man among men
I hope I can see
a man among men
how proud I'll be

Tina Teeter
Salt Lake City, UT

To my son, Donnie Teeter, who grew to be a man among men and a great ship engineer. You are my inspiration for this poem. May you touch the lives of everyone you come into contact with the way you have touched mine. All my love, Momma. Also, a special thank to Sarah Woolley for helping me with this publication.

The Pickpocket Flies

The hustle and the bustle begins before the sun rises
Ears connected to other worldly voices
Rushing passengers speaking to someone not there
Eyes pining for metal rockets that will fly them to other worlds.
They cannot see past the destination, but she is not blind
She's as quiet as a mouse
Little paws dipping deftly into deep pockets
Her fingers, specialized magnets, attracting:
Green papers with faces,
Shiny silver dimes and nickels, copper pennies,
And limber plastic cards that flip back and forth over the line of debt and
wealth.
She dances nimbly through the crowds to music born in her ears
She is a pilot in a sun-colored crop duster plane
Her aviator jacket crinkling like water across thirsting ground.
Spins and spirals looping the clouds
Deep dives and rises to come back up for air.
The flight ends when the rush is gone
And the people have flown away in their rockets.
Slim picking, her catch laughs at her and she grounds them in her fist
The sun is still up—more rockets will come, and the flight can begin
again.

Kelsey A. McCain
California, KY

*I am from California, KY, but currently live in and attend Murray State
University. I am in my junior year of studies working on a veterinary tech
degree. I took a class in creative writing, which I love, and half of the semester
was focused on poetry. This poem was an assignment for that class. After
writing the poem, I felt good about it and shared it with my family. With
their encouragement, I submitted the poem and now it is published. I am
excited and thankful for the opportunity to share my poem. Hope you enjoy!*

Scream

Hear me scream
in the silence of the night.
See me cry
in the absence of light.
Watch me hurt
as you have before.
Feel me tremble,
I'm so cold.
Taste my kiss
one last time—
One last time, like you mean it.
Take my hand
one last time,
before I can't feel anymore pain—
before my scream is silent at last.

Kasey Clark
Chico, CA

I wrote this poem during high school when I was depressed and considering taking my life. I wrote poetry to help get things off my mind. Poetry was my outlet, my go-to "counselor." I am so thankful that I am still alive. My advice—don't give up on life or people in your life. You never know what surprises life will throw at you. I would like to dedicate this poem to my mother because without her supporting me through my struggles, I would not be where I am today. I love you, Mom, and thank you for everything.

Love Shouldn't Hurt

I love you like the
sand loves the sea
I love you like the
stars love the darkness
in the sky
I love you like the
grass loves the rain
I love you like the
sun loves to shine
upon the earth
I love you more
than anything in this
world
Why can't you love
me the same
way
and stop abusing
me?

Regina Barreras
Tucumcari, NM

A Sailor's Rhyme

As we all know
there are sayings that go
that predict what the weather will show.

Red skies in morning
sailor's take warning
red skies at night
sailor's delight.

If this rhyme be true and
not just a poetry line
we then may plan for the day
be it rain or sunshine.

If rain it will be
then indoors we stay
and plan for the day.

If sunshine it be
then outdoors we stay
and plan for the day.

Sailors we know
keep their eyes on the sky
as they sail on the oceans below.

Red skies in morning
sailor's take warning
red skies at night
sailor's delight.

Jean M. Peterka
Galesburg, IL

Almost Over!

I'm on my way home
Never again will I roam

Reminds me of a lonely, old song
I've been gone for far too long

I don't know how to live free
I'll give my best for all to see

My future is looking really bright
Hope my feeling on this are right

Nights seem to be long these days
I dream of freedom in many ways

Once they let me out of these gates
I hope I can forget all of my hates

David D. Brown
Iowa Park, TX

Forgotten Stickers

I stare at the blotchy mirror,
The blemishes resembling shapes of forgotten stickers,
And reject the eyes that dart back at me.
Like daggers, they stab at my heart.
Those eyes, those same exact eyes,
Have, for sixteen years now, locked onto me.
But for only two years have they truly glared.
It has been two years;
Two years since I started being ashamed of myself,
Two years since I started changing who I was and forcing the same,
And two years since I contemplated shutting those eyes forever.
But now I have traveled far,
And my torturous setbacks have become my greatest triumphs.
I have looked into many mirrors—
Flaws from forgotten stickers in sight—
Without fear, fear for the man staring back in my direction.
I instead glance and see the real me:
Four years of age and garbed in blue overalls
Which cover a young, slim body.
His beautifully radiant smile gives light
To the world's darkest corners.
He forgives me. He loves me. He is not ashamed of who I came to
be.
Underneath all the layers, all the masks that hide my true identity,
The mud and grime that societal views have forced me to cover him in,
He is not my fear, he is not my nightmare. . .
He is my rock bottom.

Ben Zucker
New York, NY

Think About It . . .

Life is like a giant fish bowl. . .
with we just as tiny grains of sand.
Our minds, our dreams, seem limited to
treasures we sculpt with our own two hands!

We rise up every morning,
with hope sprung eternally new,
that we can capture a measure of happiness
that we all hold to be our due!

Things may seem so cloudy—
Some days, they surely do.
Then comes a ray of sunshine,
And everything seems like new!

It's hard to know the right path;
sometimes, we trip and fall;
but something will keep us going,
if we listen and heed the call.

It isn't always pleasant. . .
at times, we don't understand;
we feel hurt and doubt and loneliness. . .
yet, we must all firmly stand.

We must be the best we can be,
Must hold our head up high,
and trust the One Who can guide us—
that loving Man up in the sky.

Ruth Riese Sutton
Baraboo, WI

Heart Love Thorn

I'm the heart of love, that runs through a river
My love, sit among the one I am missing down below
next to the river flow
Console me with your love once more
until my soul is resigned
Dilate my horizon for my eyes to see
the thorns of love have just now begun to grow
breaking free from all that I know
My lips are wet with the taste of peppermint
turning those thorns into honeycomb
The terrain of the one I missed, grounded below
My heart skipped a beat some time ago—
the heart love is now scanning trying to find his next soul
the heart love is now running wild
shadowing all that compile to his will
The aroma of sweet raspberry and tangerine
dripping from the tree. . .
Where is my heart love thorn
the one I wait for? What can he do for me?
He follow my footprint of thorns and walk with me—
with no regrets, the heart love thorn has now been complete.

Adgie S. Garrett
Marianna, FL

The Answer

Did you ever feel like you were at wit's end
   Not knowing which way to turn?
Have you ever been tired of your hum-drum days
   And fulfillment is what you yearn?

There is One Who cares and One Who shares
   He knows just what is best;
His Word is so true, the words are so new
   He will give you such sweet rest.

This One is my Lord, so faithful is He
   The Bible is His book—
Such precious thoughts contained therein
   If you will only look.

Such joy to behold as the pages unfold
   His promises can be so sweet.
Your life becomes new in all that you do
   So come and sit at His feet.

He longs for you to completely rely
   On Him for your every need,
So feed on His Word and be assured. . .
   Blessings come in following His lead.

Janet C. McClintock
Bluff City, TN

I am a seventy-six-year-old wife, mother, grandmother, great-grandmother, and sister. I was inspired and prompted by my Lord and Savior Jesus Christ to write the poem "The Answer" because He and His Word, the Bible, is the answer to all of life's trials and tribulations, and brings about all joy and peace. This is my witness for the Lord. He is very personally in my heart and life and has been since I was six years old.

This Is the Day

The mighty oak sways in the evening breeze,
The birds are singing sweetly in the trees.
This is the day that God has made,
I rejoice in the cool of the evening shade.
Oh, how beautiful this earth of Thine,
When I bask in thy Holy Love sublime.
Thou hast created all things for Thy good,
Thou hast made all men to dwell in brotherhood.
Thy beauty is everywhere I look,
I see Thy reflection in a small still brook.
The beautiful flowers reveal Thy glory divine,
Their sweet fragrances makes my heart strings twine.
The hills are singing Thy songs of praise,
As they drink in the sun's gentle rays.
The rivers are filled with waters so sweet,
And the land gently rises where the mountains meet.
The snow-capped mountains glisten so bright,
As they reach with their peaks to the sky.
The prairies are filled with golden grain,
And soon it will be harvest time again.
Oh, Father in Heaven, so Holy and Divine,
Thank You for this day and this time.

Bill England
Lebanon, MO

As a small child, my mother taught me nursery rhymes. Maybe this is the reason I have always loved poetry. God and His glory, the beauty in His creation, His love in sending Jesus to die for our salvation, family, friends and love of life have all been been my inspiration to write. As a pastor who loves people, I like to encourage and help others to see and know the love of God for themselves. My wife Hazel and I have one son, two grandchildren, and two great-grandchildren. We soon will be married sixty-two wonderful years. God bless all of you.

A Poet of Little Fame

I am a poet of little fame—
no one even know my name,
or from whence I came.
Pen in hand, I wrote a line
and then one more to rhyme,
and done in a short time.
Neither a cerebral poem,
nor about family or home,
nor a lengthy tome.
It was written just to see
if a poet I could be—
or if it was just a novelty.
The words flew on the page
as my brain started to engage,
and I knew I was on a pilgrimage.
Writing soon inflamed my soul,
causing me to lose self-control,
as I embarked on the writer's role.
Writing with what I perceived as wit,
it sometimes ended up the opposite,
and at times made me want to quit.
It matters not, as I write to write—
and though I am a neophyte,
one day, my poems may excite.
Until that time, I shall remain
just a poet of little fame.

Jeannie Gudgeon
Tomahawk, WI

The Candle of Life

The candle of life is but a glimmer now
Flickering before the darkness
The cocoon sensing newfound spring
Discovering a generation of monarchs

Soon, the permanent peace will come
And shed the chrysalis of life
The metamorphosis through wormhole to butterfly
I will take flight into a new beginning
Leaving behind all earthly pain and escape

Van L. Montavon
Greenville, CA

Ernest Hemingway Speaks

Ernest Hemingway speaks;
Even the fish he hunts are willing to listen before they die.
His voice has imagination,
His beard is arrogant—
Many are jealous of this outspoken man.

Rita Greco
New Kensington, PA

The Sea of Dreams

I sat on my winding staircase looking out to the sea
I wondered why my mom would never let us be
I know that he needs me
She wants me to see what her heart seas in thee
By day, I must stay
But by night, I pay
For my heart longs to be with thee
But she locks the door
And tells me to see you no more
Yet I still sit and long for you upon this pier
I whisper to the wind hoping it will find its way to you, my dear
As I walk home, I feel fear
As I run to my house, I see your truck
I figure you had no luck
But as I walk in, I hear laughter
My mom looked at me and said, I hope you live happily ever after
You walk over to me and grab my hand as my face gleams
Then ask me to live happily ever after with you on the sea of dreams

Alice Marie Akien
Magness, AR

Catch Me, If You Can

The night lights are out
Frightful, it's not
It's cozy and rosy by the night light
Bright in my eye
Flash of light was a firefly
High above my eyes
Shy, it was
Reach, screech. .the firefly
Frightened by the unknown
Scurried away
Let it be
Sit—may I wonder
Under slumber
I dream a beam of fireflies
Fly: millions in her eyes
Sounds like thunder coming her way
Clock sounds off and awakes from slumber
Sorting what is real
She rolled over to nap some more, and drowsy she was
Tore sheets in flight, and a terrible sight
She showered and shook
Took another look
Wrote another book
Stand, Firefly, was the book
She caught a firefly in her hand while she stood on the land
The wings of the firefly fluttered away

Desiree Y.B. Eakle
Honobia, OK

Blind Love

Sweet lover, beautiful maiden of mine
how can I possibly praise your grace?
One hand to trace your gently curving spine
Or the soft complexion of your face?

My love burns like the sun that warms your hair
And wind that carries warbles under wing.
But none of these can nearly quite compare
to tones of joy, of flight you laugh so sings.

The strength of your feeling is ever-felt
With senses so tender; touch , scent and ear.
Though my eyes stare, long by your side I knelt—
As your own skies opened, felled the first tear.

My wind, my sun, my song are you to me;
It matters not my eyes are blind, you see.

Gabrielle Osborne
Virginia Beach, VA

Untitled

A voice of celestial glory
where an orchestra of candles
light the celestial deep

Awaken the angelic choir
Sing and join with a new voice
clear as Gabriel's trump

Power to shatter dark's fragile chains
Glowing rays of peaceful light
Weaving calm, warmth for a precious child

I rest at last with a song of joy in my heart
My work with you is done
and now I sleep, my precious little one

Berlinda Hebdon
Riverdale, UT

Clothes

From the store,
To the washer.
In the closet,
and on the floor.
You can never have too much—
And you always want more.

Jenna Brekke
Thief River Falls, MN

Best Friends for Life

We are friends
I got your back
You got mine
I'll help you out
Any time!
To see you hurt
To see you cry
Makes me weep
And wanna die
And if you agree
To never fight
It wouldn't matter
Who's wrong or right
If a broken heart
Needs a mend
I'll be right there
Till the end
If your cheeks are wet
From drops of tears
Don't worry
Let go of your fears
Hand in hand
Love is sent
We'll be friends
Till the end!

Joshua Dale Hunt
Worcester, MA

Sandy

She came with a blow,
A boom and a splash—
Destroying houses,
Beaches,
Cars in a dash.
She knocked over trees,
Brought death to are path. . .
Took away power,
Left cars with no gas.
She flooded the streets,
Leveled fear to its highest peak;
Spoiled our food,
Cold showers,
No heat.
Straight tragic,
No sleep—
But made us become one,
In a time of need.

Geneva Houston
Staten Island, NY

Five-Year-Old Blast

You fly in the door
light chasing, catching
each blond-white flip of hair.
Play and friends await outside
as you storm past me—
a streaking fury full of thirst.

Sweatsmells stain sweetly the air
in your wake; oh, busy boy,
oh, five-year-old blast.

Faucet roars a flood
as greedy gullet spills
steady trickles to slide
from chin to chest.

Swallowed balls of air sound
gulps and pants and gasps
as thirst is slain!

Out again, you swirl.
The faucet drips,
cabinet doors gape wide,
dirt-prints paint your presence,
faint aroma of you lingers sweaty. .'til

The slam-bang door startles me
from the survey of your blast!

Florrie Belle Britton
Littleton, CO

The Fit of Fifty

I sit
I sit
Wondering where I fit
Not with the old, like I'm sometimes told—
Thought of grave-shopping leaves me cold.
Not with the young, I can't see myself on a beer run. . .
Everything just for fun.
I sit
I sit
Wondering where I fit.
This time is uncomfortable for me;
Maybe I'm looking too hard for something that fits like a tee.
Wonder I may, but the fact I must adhere. . .
I fit in this time: today, tomorrow and, God-willing, next year.

Donna Hartney
Oakwood Hills, IL

Uniform of Consciousness

What do we base our repulsions on,
Where does the path lie?

Should we be conscious of our fellow man,
Or just watch him die where his anger lies?

From guns, drugs and sins out of hand,
The homeless, troubled, ill, uneducated,

Overpopulated and political unrest,
The mitigation of people trying to find
Themselves in a troubled land. . .

How can I help my fellow man?

The colors of a rainbow are mixing together,
Old traditions mixing with the new.

Can we settle down to worldly people,
Or will it always be out of hand
Because of a narrow-minded few?

Too much prejudice, stirred by politicians,
Carried out by news reporters, to cause unrest.

How can I help my fellow man?

If the political scene were inspired by God
Maybe we'd be close to an answer.

Let's all pull together, to see if we can, be
The people as one face, to live in our democracy.

S. Carol Kilgore
Columbus, NE

In 1992, I walked the streets of New York, Times Square. "Uniform of Consciousness" are the feelings of the streets expressed poetically. I saw diversity: people of all faces, colors, races, religions, problems, rich and poor. I hope my poetry will enable me to continue to write and enjoy New York. I have three grown children and three grandchildren. I am proud of them and enjoy writing about them.

Fancy

"Fancy" was five
with her hair in her eyes,
as the wind blew free on her knees;
the swing that she sought
her daddy had bought,
hung on the limb of the tree.
She would swing higher
and never would tire.
When the sun in the sky was ablaze,
she scrubbed her feet in the dirt;
all the birds were alert,
this was good, old summer days.
Her puppy would stay
in the yard as she played
and nip at her tiny toes.
She would squirm and jump down,
then walk around to the bush
that held the pretty red rose.
She knew not too touch,
the thorn was too much—
It would stick and make her cry.
She had a hunch,
with Mom making lunch,
it was back to the swing with a sigh.
So Fancy was five
with her hair in her eyes,
and the wind blowing free on her knees. . .
the swing that she sought
her daddy had bought,
and it hung on the limb of the tree.

Betty Goins
Cleveland, TN

Don't Count Me Out

Lord, I've struggled all
my young life; I needed
someone to take time with
me, to help me learn.

I wanted to be smart, but it
seem it never came to my turn.
Everything seems so hard for me
to understand. I just didn't know
where I could fit in in this
hustle and bustle life—all those
around me learning, doing different
things, writing books...so smart.

But let me tell you what has happened
in my adult life: I prayed, cried, I prayed
and asked Jesus to come into my heart.
He heard me—now, I'm used for His glory.

Janie Aker
Calhoun, GA

Twilight Has a Touch

The hours of daylight fade away
remembered are the hours
Included sometimes, wind and chill
perhaps some lovely shower

But now we gently come to know
before dark enters in
A cloak surrounds your shoulders now
the twilight must begin

When wrapped up in the twilight cloak
there are no shadows there
The not-forgotten times and hours
come back because we share

A softness in its gentle way
how wonderful to know
The magic of these twilight hours
good memories seem to grow

While clothed in twilight for this time
the world seems far away
How wonderful the twilight comes
a precious part of day

Just past the twilight, minds will sleep
remembering with ease
These perfect moments build a charm
Do come and join me, please

Walter Strippgen
Boulder, CO

My Forever Wife

We both played the games that no one wins
Wasn't it hard to confess our sins?

Fate brought us together
Deep down inside, I knew it was forever

But uncertainty is in us all
Especially when we've been hurt by a fall

Time to reflect on my life, that was the key
Love came back and found me

You are the force of my life
You are my friend and lover, my forever wife

Tom Briesemeister
Franklin, WI

I retired in 2010 after selling my transportation business. I have dabbled in photography and have been an artist for the past forty-five years, entering numerous shows in Wisconsin and Illinois. The poem was written several years after Pat and I were married. The poem deals with the search to find your one true love. We both experienced divorce and relationships that seemed to go nowhere. We dated, went our separate ways, and then got back together again and eventually married—both of us realizing that we finally had found our soulmate for life.

Love Never Fails

Love is patient and kind
Defers anger, puts up with the unfavorable for long periods of time
Love is not jealous, not envious on what others have
But full of service, Love does not boast nor brag
Love is not arrogant or prideful, does not act unbecomingly
Or improperly
Love does not self-seek
Love is not easily angered
Love does not take into account a wrong suffered
Love thinks no evil, Love does not rejoice in unrighteousness
But with the truth, Love rejoices
Love keeps no records of sin
Forgives, covers them up, never to be brought up again
Helps in dealing with the consequences that may arise
From past sins, Love goes through the bad times
Love is trusting and trustworthy, is not pessimistic
Love hopes, expects the best, is optimistic
Even when
Life seems to be a burden
Love doesn't quit, Love keeps going
Love grows, endures, never stops—and with Love, all is well
Because Love never fails

Mikial L. Corley
Orangeburg, SC

Our Father's Tears

As Jehovah looks down
From Heaven above
At this earth He created with love,
His eyes must be filled
With tears that He shed—
But what does He see, instead?
He sees His earth polluted and filled with hate;
It truly is a sorry state.
But as He wipes away the tears,
We get rid of all our fears.
What does He see?
Almost six million people keeping their integrity!
They have washed their robes and made them white,
And that must give Him much delight.
He knows they must of obeyed His laws
And gotten rid of most of their flaws.
Soon now, the earth will be restored;
And by all creation, You will be adored!
No reason to cry or ever be sad—
We have all come to love You,
And we are so glad.
Soon now, fulfillment of promises grand. . .
In Your new world, we all pray we stand.

Mary G. Youngblood
Yreka, CA

I am proud to say I am eighty-two years old. I am in pretty good health and, as you know, I love God and those I know. I have a cat; her name is Kitty Cat and, I might mention, she is spoiled. I have lived in northern California all my life, and I view Mount Shasta each time I go to town. I give praise and a special tribute to our Grand Creator when I see the beauty of it all.

Storyteller

If I do not have a story
spinning in my mind,
there is an emptiness in me
of an unusual kind.

Like a fire that begs for
kindling so to shine,
or the star that yearns to fall
to leave her silver line.

But when my story fills the page
my heart begins to dine,
to dance, to sing, be giddy—
her story is her wine.

Tom LaPointe
Albany, WI

My Distant Lover

Close your
Beautiful eyes
My love
Open wide
Your loving arms
Pretend
I walked in
My wondrous
Love
Giving you
A tender hug
You have
A hold
On me
Until
We meet again
Keep me
Near your heart
Always
Lover

Yolanda Elder
Los Angeles, CA

Love is the greatest gift God has given us. I'm thankful I can put His love in words. I livesin Los Angeles as a single parent of three with children. The many blessings in life inspire me to write, write, write.

Black Insanity

Black, just black.
Surrounding, trapping, choking blackness—
Blinding, dangerous blackness.
Never leaving, everlasting.

Questions fly, thoughts disappear,
Leaving me with nothing...
Nothing more than the suffocating blackness.

But then, in the black of night,
The boy so young, yet so wise;
The boy so pure, so breathtaking.

The questions gone, the sanity returning.
The pure, wise, breathtaking presence of the boy—
My heart leaping, pounding, yearning for the boy.

Through the city, by the fields,
Across the country, under the sea,
Around the world, over the sky, I chased.
I chased him, I chased him. . .
I called his name, I ran and ran,
But he was ever so far away.

And that's when I saw the other girl,
And black returned again.

Haylie S. Peacock
Columbia Falls, MT

The Life Inside the Flames

What could it be? Could it be a car into a tree?
Could it be a house on fire, or a C02 alarm with a bad wire?
As I get ready, I stand unsteady
With the thoughts and fears of what I might hear.
As I arrive, I see the fire alive.
As I move through the first floor, I break down a few doors. . .
As I break down the door, I hear a loud roar.
It's collapsing like a deck of cards,
I run very fast and hard.
I think of what might happen; I stop in a sudden reaction.
I hear a faint voice of a child, I turn around without a smile.
I look, I search so very hard, with nothing else to be heard. . .
There it was again, so I gave a big grin;
I see the child all buried in a pile.
She's, okay so I clear the way.
I make it to a door with an unsteady floor.
There's help for the girl, so I turn back to do more;
As I put out the fire, I grow very tired.
As the fire goes out, I hear a loud shout—
It's the chief to all of our relief.
I walk with our dignity and pride,
With a fellow firefighter by my side.
As we leave the scene, I bow my head and silently pray:
Thank You, God, for the help You gave us today.

Karingtin Rodgers Sklodowski
Lilly, PA

Poem of a Poem

Poems are good, poems are great,
Poems are things to appreciate.
We write them, we read them...
We really, really need them!
No, please take a note:
Sometimes they rhyme, sometimes they don't.
Bios! Quatrains!
Some poems are colorful as paints!
Poems are happy, poems are sad;
poems are exciting, poems are glad!
Most have topics, like being happy or sad.
Some can be about being reunited with your long-lost Dad!
One poem's about a star. . .
You can make a poem about a shiny, red car!
Poems are from any place, from here to there—
Some are from the center of the earth, to up in the air!
A famous poet is Dr. Seuss. . .
You might find a poem in the daily news!
There is nothing like a poem;
They're older than ancient Rome,
They were here in caveman times.
They're paragraphs with lots of rhymes!
Couplets! Triplets! These poems are really cool.
To not like them, you'd have to be a fool.
Please, take this to your home...
Please, enjoy "Poem of a Poem."

Mic Bredeway
Holland, MI

Acceptance

Different cultures across the globe
Our world's a sundry place
Many religions and customs
Diverse ways to embrace

Ethnocentrists disturb the peace
Differences they berate
Prejudice like a cancer grows
Elitism spreads hate

Tolerance the only answer
Mankind must stop the fight
All creeds and races of this earth
In harmony unite

Emily Krusos
Huntington, NY

The Wall

The wall hit the Earth with a sudden jolt,
For the Earth was weak,
But the wall was strong.
The Earth had a crack,
For that was how it was created;
But nobody knew, yet everyone did.
The wall was solid,
For it had strong structure,
But nobody noticed—yet, they were all thankful.
The people hurried. . .
For the Earth was only noticed,
But they couldn't see the wall.
The commotion distracted them surely,
For it was sure chaos—
But still, it sat there silently, waiting to be seen.
The Earth was weak,
For the wall was strong;
But a glance was never given.
The structure was meant to be switched,
For it was meant to be opposite,
But the balance was wrong.
The wall would never be noticed,
For they can't see how stable it was.
But it still was not the Earth...so, no one seemed to care.

Caroline Hallie Stokes
Firestone, CO

Lone Leaf

I swallow the fresh scent of the frost perched on the colorful leaves
I shiver as the cold needles dig into my freezing skin
I watch as the lone leaf twinkles down on its ballerina toes
It flips, flutters, and eventually falls

Lines of age
Etched into the unique physique of the leaf
I reach out and grab the floating masterpiece
Birds chirp their usual song
The frogs croaking their conclusive calls
Raucous screams of the freezing newborn

The biting wind chokes my toes
Amber-colored shafts of trees exploding out of the ground
Spears of sticks embedded into sodden kaolin-covered ground
Blades of dead grass plunge into nothingness
Waiting for the time when then they will plume with triumph

There is the solitary leaf sitting on the inky surface of the road
I glance over to the empty arms of the trees reaching into the sky
This lone moment represents
The
Turn
Of
The
Seasons

Gibson Lee Harnett
Yarmouoth, ME

A Walk in the Woods

The crescent moon
Like a Cheshire smile shines upon me
Alone I stand, bathed by the light
This light is seductive
Coaxing me into darkness
The stars shine amongst it, drawing me in like bedroom eyes
My body is surrounded by its warmth
Encasing my body in its being
"Oh, Crescent Moon, how I envy thy light
Shall I never shine like you?
I long to reach you, Crescent Moon
My lover, my savior, my friend"
And I stare into the eyes of the glowing crescent moon
As it holds my heart close to it
And flies amongst the stars
Every night, tears are shed in mourning
As the crescent moon's beauty is plagued by morning

HarleeRay Beth Bicknell
Huntingburg, IN

The Dust of Dreams

I must wait for sleep to find me, to find some rest,
while the sun retreats to her dwelling far west.
Like always, he will not find me 'til late in the night
until my eyes see the first rays of early morning light;
then, in the land of dreams, I become a welcomed guest.

In that other plane, never does one argue or protest
with the lack of worry and the removal of stress.
But before I can voyage there to find great insight,
I must wait for sleep to find me.

A sleeplessness waits each night that I cannot contest,
delaying me from gazing upon the end to my quest.
The guardians of the realm are almost in my sight,
but the rage of the Sandman I once did incite;
since from his grasp no magic dust can I easily wrest,
I must wait for sleep to find me.

Bob Charney
Berlin, NJ

The Fence

I glare, fixed gaze, split rail,
Then to what would it prevail?
All alone standing the time test,
Borders and boundaries it does suggest.

No allowance for free-thinking men;
To feel alive is mortal sin.
Rules and regulations hinder my creativity,
Tangle the thoughts and hamper harmony.

Nature nullifies but it takes time—
Our abuse, absurd as a paradigm.
Destructive and deceptive with no foresight;
Paragon of pride, an ignorant erudite.

Any answer to this complex enigma?
Pernicious parasite is the human stigma.
Nature has no hope; I sense
The ugly power of a fence.

Douglass Andrews
Julian, CA

Life Is a Song

Life is a song
Of many stanzas—
Some short and some long—
Sung as we live it,
Day by day, whether it be
Short, or very long.
In it, comes sweetness,
Joy, and love. .sometimes,
Hurt and sickness.
Yet, it is a song—if not
Sung word by word, it's
Never completed, and the
Great A-men can never come. . .
And we meander through life,
And never really live.
For life is a song; if not
Complete, it can never reach
Its true crescendo. . .
And the angels cannot sing.

David S. Edwards Jr.
Union Bridge, MD

Dad

You were my rock
You kept me strong
Told me what was right
And told me what was wrong

You were my teddy bear
To hug and to love
You were my crying shoulder
When what I went through was rough

You were my comedian
A pretty funny one, too
You always made me smile
Especially when I felt blue

But most of all. . .

You were my dad
I can never bring you back
But I have learned from your words
And, with that, I will stay on track

Amber Holbrook
Manchester, IA

Lynched

There you are—
Just six inches from me.
You look peaceful.
Aside from,
Of course,
Your snapped neck
And your limp body.
And I wonder if maybe
Someone could have
Saved you. . .
Or maybe, even, if
I could have saved you?
I watch you, and
I wish that I could
Somehow allow your
Bones to mend
And fresh air to creep
In and out of your
Defeated body.
But I couldn't save you,
And I can't save you—
Because I'm about
Sixty years too late,
And you're merely
A picture in my
Ninth grade history book.

Ana Lanfranchi
Atlantic Highlands, NJ

Wish I Had Taken Time. . .

I was so busy throughout the day,
I never took the time for you and me to play.
When you brought things to me,
I told you, "Not now." As I would clean and cook,
I often wouldn't even take the time to read you a book.
I'd tuck you in the bed at night,
Giving you a kiss and telling you not to let the bed bugs bite.
Too quickly, I'd pass through your door—
I should have stayed just one minute more.
Life's way too short, each year just flies past;
My little boy has grown up too fast.
No longer playing by my side,
He's not there anymore for me to nurture and guide.
The books and toys are all packed away,
No longer does he ask me to play.
No precious bedtime kiss between you and me. . .
All of that is in the past and belongs to a memory.
My days once busy are now too calm;
The hours are empty and way too long.
I wish I could go back and do all the things you asked me to,
Just to spend more time with you.
I'm sorry I didn't realize—
But that was the best time of my life.

Lisa Charlene Edenfield
Bristol, FL

Christmas All Alone

She was here last Christmas
seems so long ago
I wish that she would be
here with me
Oh, how I miss her so

I just wrapped her presents,
they're all beneath the tree
If she stays away, I can only say
no merry Christmas for me.

She wrote to me last summer
to say she won't be around
But I refused to believe it
I didn't think she would let me down

I have no one to sit by the fire
and watch the snowflakes fall
no one to kiss under the mistletoe
She had to ruin it all

So come what may, on Christmas Day
I don't want to be home
But for now, I'll manage somehow
As I spend my Christmas all alone

Joseph Domiano
Old Forge, PA

This Is for You, Grandpa

This for you, Grandpa
For all the times you've helped me, especially out of a few trees
For all the times you've walked with me
And answered my nature questions
You helped me plant seeds and helped me make them grow
The times we'd sit and talk about anything in our heads
When we'd sit and gripe about Grandma
And her overbearing, over-caring ways
When we'd sit outside and watch the sun
When a storm brews, we'd stand on the porch
And guess how bad it'd be
Or when we'd sit together, quietly absorbed in our own thoughts
You're always there for me when I make big mistakes
You're right by my side—
So caring and understanding, when no one else would come
You always had a way to make me laugh through tears
Or smile over a frown
You tell me, *Mistakes only prove how adult a person is*
And laugh heartily when I'd complain, "I hate being an adult"
Grandpa, through the years, you've never left my side
Hopefully, you never will
Knowing you, you'll always hold my hand
To show how much I admire you, love and care for you
To show how much your hugs, kisses, and our little talks mean to me
This poem's for you

Jenna Cumins
Clifton, TX

Happy Times

When the wind starts blowing
And the sky is full of snow
The holidays are coming
As you very well know
'Tis the season to be merry
As the old saying goes
And be happy from your head
Down to your freezing toes!
Merry Christmas to you
I am happy to say
Have lots of fun
On the coming holidays

Doloris Ryder
Vincennes, IN

For All of Time

To my Angel of inspiration.

For all of the times
I can feel you in my heart,
For all of times
I can here and see you in my mind,
For all the times that you have touched my soul...
For all of time! All of them times—
I will never ever let go!

Zacheriah John Casias
Denver, CO

Lost Angel

Misguided down a twisted path
You take in all the signs of different shapes and colors
But an illiterate child throws itself down and screams
Reread to comprehend, that's all we try to do
If you understand, then you can apply the knowledge
The efforts seem meaningless, though when attempts go ignored
No one else cares, so why should you bother?
Will someone please teach this child how to read?!
Abandoned in a dark and unforgiving world
Do they really expect us to survive this alone?
I would take a bet that you're in the light laughing
Deep down, they will never understand that we need our guide
What's to keep us from tripping over rocks and branches?
Soon you will be falling on your face, covered in mud and blood
This child needs first aid to disinfect the wounds
Clean and kiss every cut they have endured and be their Band-Aid
And don't forget the reading lessons!

Katherine Poage
Wymore, NE

Living in Color

A life can be a lonely road
or, it can be a fray.
It can be both up and down
or, smooth as crème français.
It can be lived in black and white
and various shades of gray,
or lived in rainbow colors bright—
it's all a choice, they say.

So, I'll choose the fancy hues
of bright and varied light.
The way that's filled with ups and downs;
oh, not in black and white.
I won't live life without the thrill
of bumps along the way.
I will feel, and laugh, and love—
And live today, today.

Kay Stephens
Demopolis, AL

Gone Is the Child

Soft is the pillow where lay her sweet head,
Soft were the words from her lips as she read.
Gentle the lap where she silently lays,
Gentle the eyes from which she did gaze.

Calm is the breeze as it flows in the night,
Calm sounds the cricket just out of sight.
Quiet were the footsteps that fell in the hall,
Quiet the love that she gave to us all.

Bright is the light that under the door seeps,
Bright are the tears a mother silently weeps.
Deep is the anger she feels in her heart,
Deep is the pain that has torn her apart.

Harsh are the hours from dusk until dawn,
Harsh is the knowledge she has already gone.
Gone is the child we held to our breast,
Gone to the grave to where she will rest.

Edward Eugene Simpson
Wichita, KS

Sadly Spoken

I see you there now—
It doesn't seem true.
I try to hold back the tears,
But they keep on coming.
I feel like I'm stuck in a nightmare,
Yet no one gets me out.
The line between reality and dreams
Seems to disappear more and more every day.
Sometimes, I can't find the difference
Between reality and imagination.
I remember when we would hang out and have fun.
You were like my big brother.
You guided me when I wrong
And helped me up when I fell.
I can't believe you're gone. . .
I get scared sometimes, because I can only remember you vaguely.
This doesn't seem true,
But I know it's real—
When the pain won't go away.

Desree Urrutia
Pasadena, TX

Dear Beloved, Until We Meet Again

In loving memory of D.A.B.—Missing you every day, until we meet again.

I know you feel you have lost me today,
and will know me no more hereafter—
but the truth is, my beloved one,
I live on in your smile and laughter.

Our memories and moments follow me where I must now go,
but, my beloved, it is my love for you I pray you always know.

So now in the loving spirit's embrace,
I hope you see a fulfilling life through. . .
and know, always, my loving arms wait for you.

Jacqueline Rose Bouchereau
Springfield, MA

He's My Superhero

For better or worse, marriage to you was a curse
My son always came first. One day, he'll grow up to see
right through you and your love that's forsaken—
I pray his eyes are awakened to the games your playin'
And I'm just sayin', there's no way I'm giving up on my boys.
Make plenty of noise, I'm not going out without a fight;
I taught those boys everything worth something is worth a fight.
Now who's going to keep there hitting and pitching right?
Boys and me are tight, and I'm the one who gives him eye kisses.
And why he's a superhero?
I love my son, and for him, I owe you.
He makes my rainy, cloudy days turn sunshine-y blue.
I hope he never forgives you. . .
playing with his heart should be the ultimate sin to you.
Now I see the true you. Worry not; unlike you,
I wont expose you, I'll keep that between me and you.
You and your lawyer keep running me through the ringer,
But you can say little to my middle finger:
You said love was the key, then changed the locks on me.
Your counterfeit love now don't concern me;
only God can judge me, we don't need a judge or jury.
Tell that to your hillbilly attorney.
For me, you should do the right thing:
Pull the knife out of my back and let me be a father;
instead, you twist and push it in further.
Why you bother, siding with a lop-sided grand-father?
Treason and betrayal must be the price of admission
And you keep insisting you have a heart, that hopeful wishin'.
Please God, let this Judge be a Christian.
"Have love for one another,"
Don't let His Bible pages come up missin'. . .
My little superhero's heart is what He's riskin'.

Jason Jaimez
Helper, UT

Jason Jaimez (*continued*)

Writing poetry for me is a way to escape judgments and openly express thoughts. Losing my dad at a young age affected my life in a strong way. I've learned to release guilt and pain through writing. I am blessed with the most loving and supportive mother in the world. Now that I have kids, I can see all the sacrifices my mother made for me. The inspiration for this poem came from a separation from a woman with whom I truly thought I would grow old. To anyone who can relate to this poem, keep fighting the fine fight of being a loving father or mother.

Forsaken

Into the darkness and out of the light,
I run away from this painful fight.
Running from this cold but not escaping,
I'm suffering from its frosty bite.
Hiding my pain, hiding my shame,
Never have felt such a terrible fright.
Will I ever be saved?
Will I ever be craved?
I'm crushed under sorrow's unmerciful might.
Will I ever stand free?
Will I ever take flight?
They've tied up my legs and cut off my wings,
Left me damned for whatever demons the darkness brings.
Forced to listen to all the songs that misery sings,
I'm forsaken with a forever-broken heart that eternally stings.

Drenched in an agony that I cannot escape,
It lingers on my soul like a pain-tainted drape.
It follows me everywhere I go, even to my dreams.
It seems nothing can make it stop—
Not even my tears, not even my screams.
Everywhere I go, I'm surrounded by chaos.
Never in my life have I felt so lost.
I'm just a part of the wind being blown like dust:
Stuck in this world, I have few to love and fewer to trust.
My strength withers more and more with every breath. . .
I suffer from a misery that I fear can only end in death.

Katheryn Ruth Morrison
Fort Walton Beach, FL

I'm a very bright and cheerful girl. Yet oddly enough, I have always been drawn to the darker side of poetry. "Annabel Lee," by Edgar Allan Poe, is a perfect example. I've always found a strange comfort in sadness, as well as an ironic beauty in sorrow. When I read a poem that is as truly beautiful as it is depressing, I start to feel a powerful emotion swelling deep within my chest—the kind that doesn't just touch, but completely embraces the hearts and souls of readers.

A Touch of God's Love

Just to hear your sweet voice again
To touch your deep-brown skin
To see your beautiful smile
My little angel
My little child

To see your face light up with joy
My little girl or boy

Holding you tightly in my arms
Keeping you warm
And safe from all harm

Your little hands
Reaching out to me for my help
To guide you on your way

As I look at you
I think about myself
And what God has in store for the rest of the way

For a mother's love is special
To her children whom she loves
It is like a tiny miracle
With a touch of God's love

Mary D. Wiley
Chicago, IL

Sonnet of Tenets

Pray, tell the story of your life, He said
To prove the quest was not at all in vain
Whilst lasting devils race inside your head
To soothe eternal, everlasting pain

And never have you spoke a single word
To life's true unencumbered pleading soul
For silence prays potent upon your nerve
Because it's Him you truly must extol

But bright eyes dim, for you did not repent
Your sins of life from which you all were born
And soon, your time on earth will have been spent
Though your trial of tries has been forlorn

So here, dark in the trenches where you weep
He's come to give to you abiding sleep

Nat-Hallie Harrod
Burtonsville, MD

I Shiver Uncontrollably

I shiver uncontrollably
Underestimating the foe I had so
Naively chosen to stand against
In my madness, I decided on a battle
In which is the end
My end.
As my body incessantly shakes
I try to grasp my hand around reality
The constant motion
One after the other after the other
Sends my thoughts to a uniform
Existence where feelings no longer matter
I stare into the depths of my opponent
Glancing down and seeing utter nothingness
My eyes—empty, but full of reflection
The ocean.
The waves, an endless movement
Wearing tirelessly down
One brutal attack after another
Filled with strength and determination
One thought in mind, and only one
Going forward.
Where that does happen to be
The sea need not care
It perseveres through time
Leaving the past behind in a fury
And creating the future in a flash.

Onie Tumel
Stafford, CT

What's the Difference?

My hair is red
Your hair is brown
Why can't I play with you?
What's the difference?

My clothes are old
Your clothes are new
Why do you stare and laugh?
What's the difference?

My skin is brown
Your skin is tan
Why do you bully and make fun of me?
What's the difference?

We may be different on the outside
But on the inside, we're the same
So, what's the difference?

Emily Nicole Spicknall
Huntingtown, MD

Fortitude

I carry little within the brackets of my lively coffin
Not much rattles within
But there rests within a small bean pod
Rising
And luck will never bring the rain
Nor commodity be given
I will not rise for sunshine
It is not what pushes me to the lid of my capture
Or to the eve-reaching space above
No, not sunshine pulls me forth
But in the darkness, where skin, bone and heart fall...I green
And virgin rise
Raise from the roots below that push me up
I, in all that is connected...am
Roots
Still and always was a part of my undying youth
And I have found no sunshine to bloom
But still, I do
My roots bring me fortitude

Ayla Dompert
Indianapolis, IN

Kites

They fly in the sky
while the wind is blowing;
all the different colors I see.
To the park we go
while watching the kites,
beautifully hung by the wind.

Sydney Light
Boones Mill, VA

My Second Love

Richard, when you first came into my life
I had basically given up
The idea of sharing my life with anyone
As our relationship grew
I realized how fortunate
I was to have found you
My love for you is forever
And I feel my life
Is now just beginning

Darlene McCall
Warwick, RI

Beautiful Brilliance

Humanity is God's greatest creation
Universal love is the intention
Awaken our spiritual energy and bring in peace and harmony
After life, there is death; and after death, there is life
A heavenly cycle without limitation
Life is beautiful brilliance.

Be kind to Mother Earth. She is the only one we have
Protect Her, love Her, and respect Her
She is beautiful brilliance.

Keep God first, and dreams come true
Move through the Universe to see clearly
After nine levels comes a thousand years of peace and
A planetary shift to where there is no space and time
The Universe is beautiful brilliance.

Look in the mirror to see the physical you
Look into your consciousness to see your higher self
Nourish your soul the way you nourish your body
And you will transcend your greatest expectations
You are beautiful brilliance.

From one cell to complex beings
We are perfectly imperfect and imperfectly perfect
We are of one existence, one love, one cosmos
Love one another with compassionate empathy, because
We are all beautiful brilliance.

Sharlene Asunta Jenkins
Scottsdale, AZ

As an aspiring poet, it can be challenging to find different inspirations about which to write. However, there is one thing that has infinite possibilities—the Universe. My love and curiosity for the Universe has inspired this poem.

Impossible Love

I look to my right, you're no longer there,
Totally vanished right into thin air—
Gone to never see until the next available date,
Despite trying to overcome the inevitable fate.
'Cause memories and histories seem to rule the block,
Making it improbable that you would let me be your rock.
I know the flame inside you just wants to fight to be free,
But I think I can change your outlook—though, you might disagree.
Is it wrong that I don't want to miss you but kiss you?
Too bad life is more than an intricate issue.
It's hard to move on and get you out of my mind,
When its with you that I really want to spend the rest of my time.
And I know you have your reasons, and I have mine, too;
It just sucks that they won't allow me to be with you.
But guess what I'm not giving up on it, just giving it time,
To see if later you and me can be our own harmonious rhyme.
Let's try to hang out soon, you seem to make the time stand still.
If not? Hopefully, I'll just see you at the next valley or hill.

Allan Elliot Hall
Fort Worth, TX

Love

Love has no greater or equal or opposite
Love has no limits or bounds or bonds
Love is timeless and contagious, and Love will never grow weary

Love will give everything, without ever expecting
or even asking for anything in return
Love will forgive time and time again and will find a remedy
when it seems there is none
Love can be blind, though Love can also do what is always difficult
Love is strong, resolute and unshakable

Love can move and inspire in ways that would otherwise be unimaginable
Love can seem to embrace a moment in time, but
Love can also make hours seem like minutes
Love will wait...and Love will always and in all ways be faithful

Love loves all: without exception, condition or need of persuasion
Love will always be triumphant over the enemies of heart, mind and flesh
Love does not chastise, and Love does not judge
Love is humble and gracious and good

If everything else should falter, then fall and fade away
There would still be as before and forever
Absolute, undeniable, ever-true, indestructible...Love

Lee Lienau
Spruce Grove, AB

Just One

If I could make just one wish,
I'd wish for so much more
Than having things and being rich
And having "friends" galore.

I'd wish for wisdom for us all
To succeed in making choices,
And stop humanity's endless brawl,
And quiet the angry voices

If I could chase just one dream,
I'd dream for so much more
Than being captain of the team
And living on the shore.

I'd dream of futures for us all,
And ways and means to get there
Without the constant, endless fall
That comes with lack of care.

If I could have just one hope,
I'd hope for so much more
Than fancy houses and fast cars,
And a giant boat to moor.

I'd hope for humanity to gain some sense
And stop destroying their Earth. . .
To start becoming much less dense,
And witness a rebirth.

Owen T. Walcott
Gilbert, AZ

In This Skin

In this skin from head to toe is all I will ever know
In this skin, I will be everything that has and will create me
In this skin, I have sinned, done things with regret
But it's this skin that I will always protect
In this skin, I was raised as prey
Never knowing there would be a day of solidarity
In this skin, I have fought and lost, but I have also fought and won
In this skin, I have hurt and I have loved
In this skin, I begin to see things with realistic eyes
To know the truth from all the lies
To know what hides deep inside
To see the mirror image of my soul
To hold on to what is known
A faith of the unseen
In this skin, I have known the troubling souls of brokenness
To see the jealous and the sick
In this skin, I have been wounded and hold deep scars
But in this skin, I have also seen humanity
A coming together for what is right, a tenderness in sight
In this skin, I will stand strong, I will challenge and I will fight
I will protect what is right
For in this skin I have seen the tattered and torn grow strong
I have seen your strength inside
It's our design
This mirror-image of mine
One of the same skin

Lillian Victoria Strom
Huntington Beach, CA

Beauty of Ethnicity

Roses are red
Violets are not
Here's my version of a melting pot
It includes many different cultures and clothes
From a great white pearl
To a lovely Spanish rose
From the Asians, for all the great food they have
To where you're considered free, at last
From the Indians and their Harajuku Barbies
To all the great food they serve at Arby's
To escargot—fried snails from France
To all the Jamaican dancers who dance
From the colors of the U.S.: red, white and blue
To, "Are you a U.S. citizen? I am, too!"
To the Latinos who climb the grease poles
And to everyone who eats fruit by Dole
Combine all of the souls of the melting pot
You will discover beautiful ethnicity —
Is it not?

Dajanyque Jcomplexious Peay
Buffalo, NY

Purple

Purple is
a bunch of grapes on a vine,
a tulip in the garden,
sun setting over the ocean.

Purple sounds like
grape juice being poured into a glass,
a gentle lullaby,
waves crashing at sunset.

Purple taste like
wine over a candlelit dinner,
Kool-Aid in my cup,
jelly on my toast.

Purple feels like
deep love from a spouse,
soothing song being played,
the sky before a storm.
Purple can soothe the soul.

Katie Larson
Sioux Falls, SD

Love Don't Love Nobody

I sit here staring and all alone
No one to comfort me or call my own
I thought you loved me all those years
I've faced the truth, and I'm in tears
If you didn't love me, why lead me on?
I could've accepted it, because I'm grown
The love I had for you was like pure gold
Suddenly, you started acting distant and cold
Get your act together before it's too late
I've waited as long as I'm going to wait
All I can say is, I really did try
Wake up now, or it will be your time to cry

Doris Walden
The Rock, GA

I was born in Thomaston, GA. My parents were the late Florien and Olin Walden, Sr. I am a 1973 graduate of R. E. Lee High School. My family has always been supportive of everything I attempt to do. My best friend Susie has always been there for me, through the good and bad times; we've been friends for forty years. This poem came to mind after a broken relationship. I didn't understand at the time; but now I've found real love, and I'm happy.

Second Chance

Trust—to you, there is no meaning,
so just stomp down on my heart.
Your lies that I continue believing
are slowly tearing me apart.
All the promises that you've made
were easily broken and crushed.
The meaning of loyalty soon will fade;
you're taking advantage of my trust.
Once again, you break my heart,
no more stitches remain.
As your girl, I did my part,
but your too selfish to do the same.
So I question myself: why should I stay,
 when I know that you're not through?
With the lies and the accusations and the promises that are fake,
you're cutting my mind into two.
I love you so much, and I thought it was true—
but now question marks fill my mind.
You've showed me the selfish and disgusting part of you,
I feel that I'm wasting my time.
I did nothing for you but give you my all,
and I expected you to do the same.
I changed my life, and for you, I'd fall;
but to you, this is just a game.
So here I am with another chance,
hoping you won't do the same.
And if you do, I swear to myself
that we will not remain.

Ellen Unique Harris
Diamond Bar, CA

The Promise

I trust my inner voice; it knows me better than anyone else.
It can guide me to the reality I most fear and yet desire.
I listen closely as it whispers small words and quiet feelings,
As it hums the tunes of breezy beaches or cries silent, faded tears.
It holds the key to my heart
And guards the truth embedded in my soul.

I release the past, and choose not to repeat or re-live it.
I think for myself
And discard harmful behaviors, relationships, beliefs.
I look to the future through the lens of my happiest day,
My greatest success, my bravest moment.
I focus sharply, memorize the view and reflect on it—often, and much.

I forgive but never forget, and I learn from my mistakes;
For I choose to flourish instead of hate, and I embrace this change.
I forgive the darkness. .and the sunshine. .and myself.
I experience the relief of letting go.

I discover my precious body, my deepest soul,
And I love myself in full measure, for I am an unrepeatable miracle.
I am a work of art, divinely created for a unique purpose. .. .
I grace this world with my presence.

Carey S. Incledon
Irvine, CA

Thirteen Little Children

There were thirteen little children, grew up on a farm
Mom and Dad were always there, protecting us from harm
Daddy, he worked very hard to put shoes upon our feet
Raised a garden and his livestock, we always had good food to eat
Momma made our clothes for us, sewing every stitch with love
Instilled in thirteen children a faith in God above

There were lots of shoes to buy—two pairs a year for each child
A pair for school and every day, a pair for Sunday morning smiles
Momma saved each shoebox and marked on each our name
Where we found something special every year when Christmas came
We'd wake up in the morning, hopeful hearts and little hands
A Christmas tree and presents, our own winter wonderland

Yes, thirteen little children with twice as many hands
We stood outside a locked door waiting on Mom and Dad
We'd line up by our ages until they'd say, "Come in"
The closeness of a family and what Santa had to send
Fruitcakes, candy, tangerines, their fragrance lingers still
Starlit eyes made of dreams, and empty boxes filled
Momma, a Christian angel, Daddy, a Godly man
Raised thirteen little children and twice as many hands

Iris Brooks
Augusta, GA

The Prodigal Sons

Their fathers, alone, each found the new ark;
With strength in purpose, they labored for land.
Their prophets foretold a dream:
All trees will ply their own route to Heaven.
The sons delivered and built the estate—
Pursuing a dream, they subdued the land.
A great nation rose and challenged the world,
Inviting the new and forsaking the old.
The dream bestowed was a fearsome burden;
The prophets were lost to men of illusions.
In valiant delusion, the nation met conflict. . .
The prodigal sons of the American Dream
Squander the fortune in forgotten purpose.
The children of war refuse their father's chimera,
Sundering the brainchild of a generation's hope.
And now, as we witness these hard times of folly,
We look to the ones who made our land great.
The breath of a great and despairing specter
Suffuses the land, passing tree after tree.
And like sapling ashes from the tangled forest floor,
And Time's mystic tree that falls and falls,
Prodigal sons of the American Dream—
And America's angry, alone without faith.
Forget not the visions of the wandering prophets,
Come home to your land. .and to your father's domain.

Richard Bryan Morse
Colorado Springs, CO

Train Ride

This train ride
sometimes long
too short for some
Please, join me
asks the child to his parents
who smile
point out the window
and leave too soon

Sit down
my love
asks the man with gray temples
to a woman who smiles
points out the window
and leaves too soon

We board alone and we leave alone
but it's a train ride
and the seat we leave is empty...
until another passenger finds it
and rides

Brian Ross Rick
Plantation, FL

Behind Those Eyes

She thinks that she can hide
behind that pretty smile
All of the emotions kept inside
it may take a while
But if you look into her eyes
you can see all of the hurt
and all of the pain
Silently at night
the tears fall like rain
wondering if it is all
worth the fight
She hides it so well
that no one can ever really tell
All behind that pretty smile
Just pull her close and hold her tight
just tell her that it will be alright
Wrapped in loving arms
to see her through the night
Her eyes, so full of questions
unspoken but true
Wanting nothing but
for her to talk to you
But give her time
and you will see all that she hides
kept so deep inside behind those eyes

Tiffany Smith
Mineral, VA

He Loves Me Not

He looks me deep into my tear-filled eyes
And with an acute face, he tells me his lies
He tells me everything I want to hear
He keeps me close, but not too near
 He loves me...he loves me not

Plays with my mind and betrays my heart
And every little lie tears another piece of it apart
He is a pernicious masquerade of countless faces
He'll take your love and soul to numerous dark places
He loves me...he loves me not

His falsifications, he starts to believe
He doesn't know himself, so how could he possibly know me?
Wearing his mask of charm, he'll put you under his spell
Then comes his other faces, which all ascend from Hell
He loves me...he loves me not

To him love is a game, nothing more
He lives off the hearts and souls he leaves broken and sore
He keeps me hanging on by a thread of lies
For his love, my heart cries and cries
He loves me...he loves me not

Anna Marie Kuhlman
Greenwich, OH

Death Did Not Defeat Me

Death did not defeat me, it momentarily slowed me down—
I came out on the other side, where my spirit now knows no bounds.
Death did not defeat me; over here, skies are fair.
The paths I walk down freely,
are filled with flowers beyond compare.
Death did not defeat me. On the contrary, it later sped me up. . .
for now my soul soars freely, behind every wishful thought.
Death did not defeat me: in way, shape, or form.
It just washed the world's pain away. .from my weary, tired bones.
Death did not defeat me, but one thing it did do
was take my physical moments. .away from all of you.
Death did not defeat me,
nor will it defeat any of you.
For death shows what we've accomplished on our physical plane. . .
what God had set out for us to do.

Annette V. Molina
Highland, CA

I began to write about who I am and what I like about poetry, then I realized that in writing this poem, I was inspired by the death of my mom. I knew I loved her, but didn't appreciate just how much until she passed on (such a cliché, but so true). There are times when I miss her; so to honor her and what she means to me, I have written words down that in turn have become poetry. I dedicate this poem to you, my mother, Margarita Carmen Yanez. With love from my heart, your daughter, Annette V. Molina.

What Comes After Winter

What comes after winter? I ask
Some say water from the melted snow
Some say animals out of hibernation
A few say caterpillars fully grown
Here and there, an anteater is named
A handful mention young ones ready to face the day
But when I look at the sky and the not-so-there sun
I add it all up and call upon the sun
To testify to my proclamation and agree with my reasoning
That after winter comes it all: spring, summer, fall and winter
A spring of life
A spring of death
And after winter came the sun
The sun, the spring and life to all

Chidinma Nwaoma Egesia
Washington, DC

I am an up-and-coming creative writer who has great (horrible) taste in movies. I enjoy playing sports like tennis and badminton...and I will never engage in sports where the balls are bigger than my fists. I gave myself the title "Animefreak," and got inspiration for this poem when watching one of my favorite animes. At that point, the muse decided to visit me, and I ended up with "What Comes After Winter." I have four sisters and a brother.

I Blew a Lot of Money

I blew a lot of money trying to fit in
Catering, partying, trying to buy friends
Foolishly seeking for attention
Putting up with strife ,too much dissension
Lavish gatherings seemed to be such a thrill
Sponsoring parties, putting off the bills
Torn in so many directions
Bullheaded when it came to receiving correction
Late nights of clubbing, hanging with the wrong crowd
Headaches, hangovers, stressing out
Spending money over here, money over there
Bank withdrawals, I just didn't care
I was told that desire was the root to evil
When it comes to money, some will deceive you
I learned to be careful who I allow into my gate
Because hands are out like an empty plate
The desire for money is why some came around
They disappeared when I was down
Like a comedy show, the situation turned funny
In my foolish days, I blew a whole lot of money

Erica Lynn Fairchild Sanders
Maumelle, AR

Cocktails for Two

The snow is falling this December
It is like the many I do remember
Beautiful and white, so peaceful and light
With someone I love, it will be so right
I want to cuddle, and be so sweetly warm
And sit and watch this winter storm

Cocktails for two, wrapped in each others arms
She loving me, and I beguiled by her loving charms
The two of us, it's a paradise, this Heaven for two
A search by a man and a woman is the best we can do
She is not perfect, nor am I—but perfect is the match
The love we have is everyone's adventure from scratch

Are the two of us destined to be together in this test?
Or, will ups and downs cause our love to rest?
No, it will never rest nor stop—this love is our bond
A lifelong joining of two people lost and now found
Of each other, built on respect, trust and communication
This bond, this love, this mate is forever, pure sensation

Duff Gray
Lewistown, MT

Rain Lover

Her heart wasn't here, she was with the rain—
She likes the smell, the relief from pain.
Her love of rain is one astonishing sight;
She will stay up for hours listening to the rain fall at night.
When the rain comes in fall,
You know where to find her. . .
She sits in the park with the angels all,
And listens to the steady heartbeat behind her.
She is a rain lover, no one can match her love for God's creation;
Her joy for the rain's peace and sound is bigger than all the nation.
I won't say her name, for it is a secret. . .
Maybe one day, you can find out her secret.
An angel on earth, some might say,
A nature lover always—by night and by day.
Angels adore her grace in the wet, gray days,
And listen to her songs in the night of the rainy-filled days.
Rain lover, oh, sweet rain lover—
Like her, there is no other.

Milla Irina Espinoza
Seattle,wa, WA

You Are Beautiful

he can't see, he is blind
you are beautiful, you are kind
your heart is light, your love is pure
so why can't he love anymore?
He is selfish, he is brute
you are gentle, you are cute
your mind can't take it anymore
he can't have you, you're too much
you are loved and not alone
your hands are always intertwined with others
but that's okay; you are sad, but that will fade in time
you're not his yin, nor he your yang
your love will not be too much for the one
hearts will hurt, eyes will bleed
don't give up, dear, just 'cause he can't see
your love is strong, your heart is pure
if he can't stand it, he's not strong
every woman needs a man that can be
your Adam, while you're his Eve
you need better, so don't look back—only ahead
for he is not your Adam or yin, nor is he using his head
for he is not a man; he is boy
I can see you happy with a man
for he is your Adam and your yin
and you are his Eve and his yang
so don't be blind like him
smile, and don't let go of hope
people love you and will help you up
take the chance, and you will see
you are truly beautiful, indeed

Krystalann Merie Chapelle
Joliet, IL

Memories

If I could see a rose
Growing near the street
As beautiful as the sky
Or two soulmates when they meet
I'd fall in love with the sweetness
Of the air as it breezes along
Or the gentle, quiet melody
A lullaby, a song
And as the people would listen
They'd feel something so pure
Yet barely there—a whisper
Or a small, mumbled murmur
It'd fill them up, it'd be there
When they were feeling weak
It'd be the best thing they could ask for
The best thing they could seek
And when the music faded away
And the love wasn't quite as strong
Those people who hadn't heard, or cared
They would be proven wrong
Because when the end got closer
The memories remained
So although some things were lost
Most importantly, things were gained

Ella Porter
Lexington, NC

I Stood a Thousand Years

I stood here for a thousand years.
By sand and wind I have been unceasingly ravaged,
But my final destruction could not have been more savage.
Even a stone Buddha can shed tears
As I fell to the sound of barbed jeers.
A peaceful sentry cut down in needless havoc.
I left my post; in its place an empty passage.
My death's knell is a thunder of cheers.
Here I once stood
For a millennia and more—
A silent, patient guide.
I would return if I could
But I was an innocent casualty of war.
Alas, I have died; I have died.

Aliza Rose Rux
Aberdeen, SD

I Speak

I remember when I was young
Hoping, feeling, believing
Things I was supposed to believe in at that time
Until I got in to the next grade

My mind got scrambled
Like eggs on a skillet during breakfast time
I was still young
But not in my mind
I was doing what I wanted to do
I didn't care what no one said, because only I knew what was true

As I grew up
I started to realize
The people I love and know
Start to die

Murdering, killing and drug-dealing
And no reason why
I can only grab my book and start to cry

I keep my cross close
And I'm proud to say
That without *God*
I would have lost my way

Ashley L. Hawkins-Williams
Kansas City, MO

Wine Drunk

It's six in the afternoon, it's six in the evening
either way, you're wine drunk and I'm punched with crush.

I think we've met before, it seems
your eyes are crooked, so are mine
But I can see, but you cannot
but you remember and I cannot.

Is it the concussions or the fear of another blow to the head?
The chest, the heart, my mind, my soul and yours

Is it love, or just another crush that smothers me
smothers a flame and grinds an ash?
It's taking names and taking mine

I remember you, your face, your name
we met once before
Why don't you remember?
I remember you, but I remember everyone—
but mostly, you.

I've done this before, I've been in love many times
Many people have tread on my heart
but I've stomped on many more

I don't want to hurt you, I never meant to hurt anyone
No one, I swear, I promise, I promise...it means nothing

Paige Alexandra Boivin
Wyckoff, NJ

Striving

You brought me
into this world
When I cried
you soothed me
When I was cold
you kept me warm
As I grew older
you were my role-model
I learned how to survive
from you—
You taught me to trust
and believe in God
You encouraged me
when I was down
You got me out of
every bad situation
You are the *woman*
the *mother* I strive to be

Marketha Bennett
Augusta, GA

Just Me

I am who I am and make no excuse,
I chose not to continue on the abuse.

I was determined to stop the family dysfunction,
before it meant my own family's destruction.

I did this all by myself, with no help at all—
even though you can't fathom that call.

I am different from you, I don't think the same;
I am not caught up in jealousy and shame.

I just chose to be the change that I needed
and don't need from you to feel you are cheated.

We make our own course through our lives—some good, some bad—
don't chastise me because you are sad.

I am happy enough with the Me who I made;
now, go out and find the You who you crave!

Lorraine Allen
Channahon, IL

Forest Song

Forest, oh, forest,
I hear your song
Beginning:
Saplings planted in
Dead of night,
Blessed to become
Giants.
Forest, oh, forest,
Such melody
You offer:
Fledglings shall
Learn to soar
High above your
Branches.
Forest, oh, forest,
What is that
Dreadful sound?
Men invade,
Strip you bare—
Leave nothing but
Loud void.

Forest, oh, forest. . .
What have we done?
Who now will hear
Your song?

Jennifer Bird
Madison, WI

Beautiful, Black Woman

What is a beautiful black woman?
She is active in the lives of those she loves
She is honorable in the way she carries herself
Her love and passion burns like the sun at its highest point
She is determined to make this world better for herself and others
The standard she has is magnificent
The drive she has is unquenchable
And the beautiful ebony skin that radiates
Shows the inner light of God in her
You are a beautiful, black woman

Gregory Marcelus McFarland
Philadelphia, PA

My name is Gregory Marcellus O'Daniel-McFarland, and I'm a descendant of many ethnic groups. I'm proud of this bloodline, and I celebrate it with my mother, brother, grandmother, sister, cousins, uncles, and aunts. We are a talented family with gifts in engineering, writing, poetry, music, and academic disciplines. I'm proud that I inherited a gift of art, which entails writing, poetry, painting, and drawing. It is also because of this gift that I was inspired by Efia King, a former schoolmate of mine, whose lifestyle and look inspired me to pen her beauty.

Struggle of Self

You say you love me,
but it's not true

You say I make a difference,
but it's not true

Drawn in by the cares of life,
I am depressed

The world is better off without me. . .
I am depressed

I am full of mistakes,
stupid, stupid

I will never get things right,
stupid, stupid

When all looks dim,
seek help

When your strength is almost gone,
seek help

Don't lose hope,
you were put here for a purpose

Press on. . .
You were put here for a purpose

You cannot change the past—
let it go, look forward

But you can choose what happens now. . .
Let it go, look forward.

Nathaniel Miller
Mount Pleasant Mills, PA

The Dream

One man don't make an army
One man don't make a team
One man can't do it all
But one man can have a dream.

He could be unsuccessful
Maybe not up-to-par
Or he could hit on something
To make him known both near and far.

One night it may come to him
Just what the formula needs
It might be in the medical field
Or in a bag of seeds.

One man built a building
One man built a machine
One man walked on the moon
Because one man had a dream.

We will get all excited
When to the top rises the cream
Look at all the great things that've happened
Because of one man's dream.

You never know when you retire at night
Just what will pop in your head
And when someone asked where it came from
Just say it came to me lying in bed.

Roger D. O'Quinn
Abingdon, VA

Not in my wildest dreams did I ever think my poems would be looked at by professional folks. I like to take a topic and toss it around in my mind—kind of like a washing machine—and wait until it's ready to write. I thought of all the poems I had written about people, places and things...but one morning at about three a.m., I awoke and "The Dream" was ready to write. God bless you as you read my work.

New Me Is Born

Fear of pain
Locks one's heart
No longer able to trust
To trust loved ones
For they have been untrue

Lies wounded me
Hate engraved and beaten into my soul
Leaves nothing left but to bleed
It's killing me inside

The new me is born
Barriers have been built
Unable to be broken down
The gate no longer open

Hiding in the farthest reaches of my mind
Unwilling to be seen
Pain is unbearable

Fear of pain overtaking one's soul
Slowly shattering wants and needs
Hopes and dreams
Lessons are learned
No reason to give in

Ashley May Clark
Forest Grove, OR

If I Could Rule the School

If I could rule the entire school
It would be totally cool
Less homework each day
School would be on Friday
I'd also build a big indoor pool
In every room, there will be an arcade
Don't have to worry about a low-grade
"Attention kids. .it's Friday
So just run, yell, and play!"
Does the principal feel betrayed?
Outside, there's bungee jumping really high
I rule the school, so I should try
It was amazing and fun
Oh, why'd it have to be done?
Then I gave my biggest sigh
Wouldn't it be really cool
If I'd rule the entire school?
The principal yelled
"Young lady, you are expelled!"
Monday, we're having a duel
What have I completely done wrong?
Everyone's had fun all along
I took a big aim
I broke the antique frame
I tried to be confident and strong

Sakshi Pankaj Lawande
Bettendorf, IA

Granny's Angel

Her eyes are bluer than
The bluest sky on a sunny day
Her hair is many shades of golden browns
She is my angel, Granny's pride and joy
She gives me a reason to get up every morning
She is truly Granny's angel
She is one-of-a-kind, and she is all mine
Her smile warms your heart, and at the same time
Her laughter fills a room with joy and happiness
For everyone around her to share
She is truly Granny's angel

Tracy J. Hill
Joshua Tree, CA

To Slowly Fade Away

Memory
Engaged, recollect
Outgoing, recognizing, gleaming
Cognizant, vibrant, lonely, forgetful
Terrifying, depressing, fading
Lost, backwards
Alzheimer's

Lisa K. Pott
Ellensburg, WA

Misty River

On the banks of the river
Mist on the rise
Feet in the water
I feel at ease

As the river flows
I let my problems go
To God, I seek
Peace of mind.

To be one with nature
And God above
To seek, I shall find
Answers to all.

Mist on the rise
As the river flows
I let go
To seek, I shall find

Teresa Lynn Lindsay
Empire, AL

A Miracle

A faint breath of life, barely visible to the human eye,
Escapes its breathtaking, fragile form;
Supple, snow-white cotton envelopes its spirit.
Soft, brown, velvety moss completely covers the frail head
Of an angel sent from above
To shed life-sustaining sunshine on the deprived souls
Of those who constantly struggle to obtain a heavenly home;
As the eyes and mouth open wide,
The small limbs of hope, love, peace and endurance
Reach and lay hands on the oppressed.
Slowly, silently the captive of despair
Is released from bondage of suffering, pain, and hate.
With a renewed spirit of love and forgiveness,
The soldier of the cross relinquishes her spoils of war,
To the keeper and protector,
Until the next victory is won.

Novella Worley Bowling
Corbin, KY

Why?

What is it that drives you
to be the greatest?
My want, your need, their force?
If only you knew—for then,
you could change.

This icy determination
pulses through your veins
like heroin to an addict.
You want more. You need more,
you force more. Pressure, always
pressure on your shoulders—
Like the world on Atlas.

The time has drawn forth.
On the saddle, helmet tight, suddenly
shooting out like a bullet from the gates.
The rush of regret. Why are You doing this?
Quick, veer right. And...silence...
A deafening silence.
No time to look at the damage.

If only you knew why.
Crossing the line,
the line of glory, or so they say.
But what you have become does not
bring joy. .rather, guilt.

Sarah Stewart
Orinda, CA

A Daughter's Farewell

They say that's Mother,
Eyes tightly shut, face so pale.
Can that be her, or perhaps another?
Thin, thin, so extremely frail.
They say *that's* mother.

Where then her angry frown,
The biting, spiteful bitterness
That thrusts and jabs 'til I'm put down?
I'm at a loss, I must confess.
They *say* that's Mother.

Her hair still shiny-white,
The busy hands so strange at rest.
Can she...awake? She *might*.
But hands crossed upon her breast,
They say that's Mother.

Just yesterday, the day before,
She walked and talked and screamed at me—
Frightened to my very core.
Now sad...relieved...I'm forced to see
My mother, dead in satin bed.

Frances Potts
Sunnyside, WA

What I See

When I look around, I see
All God's handiwork in everything.
I stand in awe and I ask how could it be...

People come and go, busy in life;
Take time to praise God for all
things, big and small.

God is my best friend—
He is one on whom I can depend.
He is always there to listen and care.

I love my Lord and know His love is endless.
I give my all in all for my Savior.
Just to see His face and walk in His grace. . .

The wait is well-worth the race.

Joyce M. Pettit
Lyman, NE

Daddy's Gone

The family's quiet,
The music stopped.
The aroma ended—
Parties, dinners, meetings, too!
Ended, gone, wiped cleaned, dead-bolted.
Belongings shared, stories told!
Pictures divided, cupboards bare;
Labored hard, love was there.
Laughter, tears, boys a-playing,
The rooms are empty; daddy's bed is gone.
January 12, 2009
Daddy closed his eyes
One last time.
Ahead of us,
Daddy's gone.
But—life goes on.
He prayed often,
He prayed long;
Salvation through Jesus,
Daddy knew
That was his hope
For each of you.
Yes, Daddy's gone,
But please live on;
Blessings shared, legacy broadens
Serving God your whole life long.
Then we will gather together
With Daddy and others,
And he will be no longer gone.

Joann Brugger
Oak Harbor, OH

Mom's Lament

With bleary eyes, I stumble into the baby's room
To comfort her in the dark.
What is it like to sleep the whole night through?
I sure need a little spark.

Up before the crack of dawn
The laundry lies before me;
The sink is full of dishes,
Why didn't anyone warn me?

There are diapers to wash,
Bottles to fill,
Floors to scrub,
A baby's cries to still.

Oh, Hubby is now home
So a meal to prepare.
Oh my, I just noticed
Dust settled everywhere.

The paycheck I receive
Is full of zeroes.
Mom's truly are
The unsung heroes.

Marianne E. Smedley
Spring Valley, IL

Moments

Right now
is a moment.
Good or bad
happy or sad
dark or light
it's a moment—
life is a collection of moments.

They create a path
and each slab of concrete we pass
is in the past.
We can't retrace our steps
we have to move forward.

Like sharks
if we stop moving
if we get stuck in a moment..
it all ends.
Life will stop.

So we move forward.
We forget
sometimes, but that's okay—

We're just learning how to let them go.

Madison Anne Albornoz
Ellicott City, MD

A Year in Review

"In time, things will be different,"
  she said as she walked out the door.
It felt like the last time I would ever
  see her in that context.
That same day, my mother came over
  and told me she was sorry.

The rain danced violently along the rooftops
  in perfect tune with my tendencies
towards her on one of my worst days.
I kept telling myself I would not stay this way,
  but I suppose that was a blatant lie;
I've grown comfortable in a downward spiral.

I called my mother again that day
  to explain to her how I felt.
All I got was familiar bitching and moaning
  and that unsettling feeling in my gut.
Later that night, I did what I wanted;
  I went to her house anyway.

The door was unlocked, an unfamiliar scenario.
  My hands were meant for savagery that night.
She was in the sheets with someone I had not seen.
  The scene played out like practiced fireworks—
An explosion of red and a puncturing gaze.
  I left before I could let it sink in.

Zach Keenum
Marengo, IL

I never really thought much of writing poetry until a few of my friends told me I was good at it. I sing and write songs for a pop-punk band as my primary creative outlet. The songs and lyrics I write are aggressive, abrasive, and intense, as I hoped this poem would convey. The inspiration for "A Year in Review" comes from a botched relationship between me and a long-term girlfriend. Everyone only talks about the shiny parts of love and never the bad—I'm a realist, and you should be, too. Find my band and my life at www.facebook.com/thisisctc.

Why I Am Afraid

I am afraid
I won't see her again.
I am afraid
She will be gone.
I am afraid
I won't be able to say
"I love you,"
One last time.
I am afraid
That she doesn't care.
I am afraid
That she doesn't love me.
I am afraid
That my mom,
Wherever she may be,
Will never get better.

Alyssa Smalley
Woodbine, IA

Cold-Weather Chores

Down the alley, restless calves are bawling
I reach for a halter and a pale of grain
Big flakes of snow are gently falling
I'm glad it's not a freezing rain

There are cows in the south pasture
They need brought to the barn
We ride our horses at a jog, me and my sister
In the fluffy, cold snow, our horses are a bit stubborn

After getting the cows through the gate
We herd them home along the fenceline
If all goes well, for supper we won't be late
Pick up the pace, you ornery bovine

It's about a mile back to the corral
At twenty-five-degrees Fahrenheit with a northeast wind,
my toes and fingers start to sting
This wouldn't be the time for a broken bosal
As prancing hooves swirl up the snow, I'm wishing it was spring.

Julie Plotts
Oberlin, KS

I grew up on a family farm/ranch in Decatur County of northwest Kansas. My mother's side of the family is from around Hayes Center, NE. I have four sisters and two brothers. My sisters and I always enjoyed using the horses for cattlework. My brothers rode sometimes. I also helped with the farming. I've always had horses. Currently, I have five, and I am training two of them. I participate in activities with our local horse club, work with cattle whenever possible, and have several hobbies. I work full-time as a certified nurse's aid at a Good Samaritan center.

An Ending

A polished stone made warm by the sun
Fingertips move along the writing
Though not the touch being sought in that moment
Eyes absorb the color of the stone
A shade for the dead
A stone
A name
A moment born
A moment died
The sum of one's life
A hand to lower a flower to the ground
A thought to the lifeless form buried below
A tear sliding down a face to fall and salt a blade of grass
A "good-bye" wrenched from a heart and thrown past reluctant lips

Carol Tierney
Manteno, IL

I Remember You

At each and every time we meet,
you say it seems we have met before.
Yes, I know and such a treat—
even though time has passed a year or more.

If you don't remember when and why,
then time has not been kind to you.
Just maybe you can remember, if you try,
and then we won't have to make such ado.

As I met you with thought in mind,
days gone by as if just moments ago.
If by choice or some chosen design
that we were to meet, someone is sure to know.

I often wondered at that special time
if somewhere in time, again we will meet.
Friendship is a choice, both yours and mine;
the seeds were sown for its roots to seat.

Although a parting of time leaves a gap,
and you find life becomes a bore,
just reach out and think of memory's map—
and again, you will open up friendship's door.

We will meet again, this for sure I know.
And all that you will have to say or do,
just let that greeting come forth to flow. . .
Hi, my friend, I remember you.

Charles K. Fletcher
Lebanon, MO

My Bed

It is the bed of a Sunday morning,
Heaped with deliciously love-tousled sheets
and blankets wrapped around arms and legs.
I roll into the warm spot left by the one who loves,
The one who has risen and returns with
Fragrant, freshly brewed gold,
Filling the shaded room with a presence,
Inviting a return to losing myself.

It is a bed of a three o'clock
with pressed sheets and chastely folded blankets
that do not tantalizingly invite,
but rather, demand party-crashing,
chaperoned by sun-washed windows,
giving me twenty stick-straight minutes
to hide from the others and find myself.

It is a bed of the darkness
With cool sheets and a warm blanket of world peace,
That plunges me into the depths of a magical sea,
Like a diver in search of treasure,
Surfacing with a pearl or a perfect deformity,
Or, at least, a preserved icon of my real self.

Ellen Bonlender
Milwaukee, WI

Let's Make a Difference

Planet Earth is the place where we live and breathe.
People don't care, so they just leave.
Some people still don't care anymore;
The planet just may feel like a canker sore.

Everyday I look up and see gray skies.
People litter, so it's like saying lies.
I wish people would stop polluting—
Instead, do the respect to the flag by saluting.

People all around the planet could make the earth less dirty;
Some people could have an idea that's nerdy.
Who care what kind of an idea somebody comes up with?
It just matters that we clean up our earth.
This could be a whole new start, new beginning, or a new birth.

Serena Wilson
Gretna, NE

Slow Down

Slow down! Listen to the music
In silence,
Dance a little by yourself;
It's okay.
Read a book, write some verses,
Relax your mind.
Tomorrow shall bring new anxieties.

There is no mountain too high
That can't be climbed;
No ocean too wide
that can't be crossed.
Smile often,
Respect all creatures
That share our earth-planet.

We are brothers and sisters
After all—
Slow down and listen to the music
Of life within,
Wherein the Great Spirit abides.

Andrew Batcho
McAdoo, PA

A Future Unknown

Bright colors, so unnatural,
Fall with every gust of wind or breath
Crunchy footfalls, so loud, so comforting
Track your every step that follows the fall
As they blow through the air
Gently brushing your face as you stall
Trying to prolong the time you spend walking,
Through the wood and the mountains
So bright, but so bare,
You stop and you stare with wonder in your eyes
And hope in your heart
Hope for the future—for surely, this beauty
This wonderful beauty, can't just go
And leave nothing behind
In the future unknown

Brianna Marie McCarthy
River Edge, NJ

Pick up the Pieces

A devilish, wounded mind, shattered innocence
Willful, senseless mayhem created cacophony
People the world over, thought to make sense
Why one demented soul wrought blasphemy

Vibrant, virgin, vital children learning the Threes
Teachers proving the known, ignorant of the unknown
We're taught to pray to the One who knows and sees
Did he believe that we had reaped what was sown?

The weapon that decimated was our empty belief
Those children are sound and safe with a familiar face
A maniacal menace dispensed an atrocity as a thief
Shaped a forsaken, barren, bloody, broken place

Sandy Hook, a peaceful, pastoral, pristine picture
Sons, daughters, brothers, sisters, nephews, nieces
Grief, guilt, sorrow has become a damaged fixture
Will we trust our forgiving God to pick up the pieces?

Lonnie Hirth
Commerce City, CO

I felt compelled to express my outrage and at the same time share my overwhelming faith, revolving around the atrocities of Sandy Hook. I must, figuratively, stamp my soul with the undying belief God and Heaven exist— because too often, we experience the bowels of Hell.

Sleeping Neverland

Sleep—a boat to Neverland,
bobbing in foaming water,
heading for a beach of sugar sand
where memories frolic amidst
a forest of imagined trees
that existed long before age,
a thieving sort of disease,
robbed you of creativity
while planting an idea seed
among those young trees
that this, you need
for your continued prosperity—
that you should feel glad to be vested
of such childish nonsense,
for once watered and rested,
that seed will sprout high
and begin to sink the island.
Then you board that boat
that once brought you to Neverland. . .
but now bears you to the edge of the world.

Devin Larain Prasatek
Rochester, MI

Daniella

First time we saw you
So tiny and new
Perfect was our point-of-view.

Tubes and wires
Blankets and lights
Two pounds, thirteen ounces—what a beautiful sight.

Your first year of life
Was a challenge for you
But you're such a fighter
We knew you'd pull through.

We loved when you'd come to see Grammy and Pop
No matter what
All else would stop.

We'd walk with you, talk to you and sit down to play
That's how we'd spend
Most of the day.

You're huggable, lovable, also petite
Last but not least
You're so very sweet.

To our little Daniella
Today you are one
We hope when you're eighteen
You're just as much fun.

Dianne Albertson
Bloomsburg, PA

I was inspired to write a poem because my granddaughter was born nine weeks early—weighing only two pounds, thirteen ounces, and about fifteen inches long. The first twenty-eight days of her life were spent in the neonatal intensive care unit of the hospital. Being so tiny and frail and hooked to all sorts of devices, I knew it would take a miracle for her to survive. That miracle happened, and I am the proud grandmother of a petite, lovable, active two-year-old.

Christmas Tradition

Snowflakes danced across the sky,
The cool, crisp air was cold and dry.
My cheeks pinked when I walked outside,
As my warm flesh and the winter air collide.

The choir chanted Christmas songs,
Singing perfectly, without one note wrong.
The streets were lit with golden lights,
Which filled my soul with various delights.

At my Grandmother's, the house smelled of gingerbread;
Newly-bought Christmas cards scattered the bed.
Cookies were frosted and the tree glowed,
Jingle bells jingled and outside, it snowed.

Santa's a-waiting away in his workshop,
As the reindeer prepare on the rooftop.
The big man will take off once all is done. . .
Twelve a.m. rang and Santa had to run.

Reindeer flew, and presents were opened;
The job was finished, and the snow whitened.
Being with family truly pulls at the heart—
It makes us realize how hard it is to part.

Just about everyone celebrates Christmas nowadays,
Between hanging tinsel, and performing in school plays.
Keep family in mind, and always be bright.
Merry Christmas to all, and to all a goodnight.

Jessica L. Hall
Tunkhannock, PA

The Hearth

Just one spark can start a blaze
The smallest flash becomes a fire
A light emerges through the haze
The scorching temple built upon a pyre

Thoughts are sparked within the mind
and from our lips take flight
One light of a brighter kind
shining through the night

Our sparks land in one another's minds
And in our thoughts find tinder
Flames grow and to ambition bind
Or fade to cold, blue cinder

Build a fire in your soul
Feed it with your passion
Let determination be your coal
And what a fire you can fashion

Create a hearth inside yourself
Welcome your fire in
Make it shine and spark with health
And find out who it will enlighten

Eleanor McLellan
Onaway, MI

Angel to Me

I hope I get
My wings one day
So I can protect you in every way

What a blessing to be able
To watch you get old
Wish I could be there
To touch and to hold
A very special person
So I am told

I believe it is true
Still wish I could be with you
But I am not
I am in Heaven looking down on you

Often, I wonder if you notice me, too
Your soft, light skin
Your beautiful, light-blond hair
And a smile that lights up the sky

It doesn't matter if you ever meet me
Just know that you are an
Angel to me

Jose De Santiago
Santa Ana, CA

Untitled

Were you alone last night
Were you thinking about me?
Did you hold a pillow tight
Did you see the waning moon?

A touch on the arm
A kiss on the lips
Your brilliant eyes

Love
Desire

A touch of the cheek
A kiss goodbye
Your courageous smile

I was alone last night
I was thinking of you
I held a pillow so tight
I dreamt of the moon

Kelly McQuerns
Austin, TX

Heaven Makes "Cents" One Penny at a Time

I found a penny today, just laying on the ground—
But it wasn't just a cent, this little coin I found!
For "found" pennies come from Heaven,
That's what my grandpa used to say.

An angel may have dropped it down
For an unexpected loved one or friend,
Hoping to see a smile where that
Pitiful frown had once been.

Intended specifically just for you,
A special gift from someone up above trying to
Say hello, cheer you up, or to say I love you!
Yes, that's what grandpa truly believed.

That those tiny little coins were dropped on purpose
To earth, for you or me to receive.
That's the story my grandpa told me
As a child, and I still believe it today!

So the next time you think this world
Is intent on dragging you down
While you're out there looking at the ground,
Please don't make a big mistake—
Pick up that penny laying there, for Heaven's sake!

For surely, now you know that penny was placed just perfectly
In your line of sight by an angel from Heaven watching over you!
Of course, this poem would not be complete
Without mentioning the penny I just found on the street. . .

Thanks for the pennies and the memories from Heaven, Grandpa.

Brent C. Schwertz
Rolla, MO

The precious, little time I got to spend with my grandparents on earth inspired me to write this poem. In our modern, busy and chaotic lives, we all forget to enjoy moments in life with family and friends—forgetting that the best things in life are free from God above, for us all to receive. As the old saying goes, "Take time to stop and smell the roses!" This truly is great advice, for we never know when our time on earth will be a faded memory—wishing we all would have enjoyed more quality time with God, family and friends.

The Death of Dreams

Close your eyes and forget your dreams;
Remember where you were, when you heard the screams.
If you move forward, just a niche in time,
Buzzards are swarming in the night sky.
Sweltering heat on the rise,
Children starving in the street with the mark of the beast.
There are storms on the Sea of Galilee,
The second coming is near.
Why all the fear on the faces of the true believers?
It's just the rise of the King of kings,
The rebirth of their dreams.
He'll look through your eyes
And, much to your surprise, you'll be left behind
With your rituals and your prayers—
Your earthly wares, your hypocrisy.
You fools, it truly is the death of dreams.
Fall in line, only the meek ill be left behind.
The cowards are among the selected few.
Does that include you, or is your heart true?
Or stained red from the womb of humanity?
I can't see, it's the death of dreams.
I can't breathe, it's the death of dreams.
I can't breathe, it's the death of dreams.
Or, is it truly the death of me?

Jeremy Lee Valdes
Clearfield, UT

I wrote "The Death of Dreams" while struggling to battle my demons. "The Death of Dreams" assisted me in finding my voice. Our dreams will only die if we let them. I pray my work will inspire everyone to reignite the fire that lives in all of us and live life to its fullest. This poem is dedicated to my mom for always believing in me, and to anyone who is or has a loved one who is an addict. May God bless us all.

Cruel World

Dear World,
The landscape and beauty is magnificent
The trees cover the surface protectively
But beneath the layer of safety is pain
There is a man who was laid-off
A widow who lost her husband
A child who was abandoned
A man drinking away his sorrows
A girl sleeping outside, alone
A hospital full of the sick
A teenager trying to belong
A girl taking all of her father's abuse
A mother who has lost all of her strength
A drug-addict, trying to get his fix
A single mother, trying to make things work
An elderly man, waiting to die
A homeless family, cold and lost
A girl who thinks the only choice is suicide
A boy who cries because he is bullied
A woman trying to cover up her depression
Why are you so unfair?
Why do you put up a façade?
Why do you let us down?
Why, World?

Sara DeZwaan
Holland, MI

Last Supper with Dad

I brought your sweater
and helped you to the table
and sat with you while your dinner was served;
but words fled like cowards, like deserters,
leaving only silence
vast and formless between us.
I learned then how little it takes to break a heart:
a glance, a gesture,
the way—
with so much lost, with nothing left—
your trembling hands
carefully set the silverware straight
and neatly folded your napkin
before you settled in again
to wait.

Nancy Grant
Centennial, CO

I wrote this poem in loving memory of my father, Marion S. Bonner, who died of Alzheimer's. To others who have lost loved ones to this merciless disease, I offer my deepest sympathy.

Open Your Eyes

Open your eyes, my friend, and see all that lies before you
Bright sunshine that comes with the mourning dew
Majestic mountains, with skies so blue
Children doing the things only children can do
And the joy of just being you
Wait, don't close your eyes
For you have not seen all there is to see
Like a puppy dog who wags his tail with glee
Or a flower that blooms with help of honeybee
Open your eyes, my friend, and I am sure you will see
All that life has to offer both you and me

Carlis Lemart Jones
Durham, NC

Disturbed

I'm running,
feet pacing as I look out the corner of my eye:
heart racing.
I'm nothing but
a lonely, black child in a cruel world of racial remarks
and let-downs of labor opportunities,
destined to find my riches
like the pretty, white kids—
whose ancestors left them loads of money.
They seem to have it the easy way, but me. . .
I struggle.

Nakia Ka'sha Sharp
Gadsden, AL

There Is a Monkey in My House

There is a monkey in my house
She hollers and screams, unlike a mouse
Oh, how she makes me crazy as she swings on the lamp
I'm starting to think I should send her to camp

There is a monkey in my home
Her curly hair, she never combs
She eats all my bananas and grows quite plump
She is a bother I wish I could dump

This little monkey is so lazy
She is starting to make me crazy
She is so rough with all of her toys
And she makes too much noise

This little monkey plays all day
She bosses me around in her own, little way
Wherever she goes, she leaves a mess
I am starting to like her less and less

Then she stops and looks around
Her catastrophe, she has just found
Her humongous mess she starts to undo
All of her messes—there are not few

I watch her tidy up and clean
Is this the same little monkey?
I can't believe what I've seen!
Then to her I call
She is my sister, after all!

Lydia Sutton
Statesboro, GA

My Senior Years

The years have passed
And I've grown old
Now I find out
What I was told
Is not the truth
So I'll be bold
And write this verse
So I can scold
The ones who knew
Words of truth untold
While a bill of goods
Dusted off and sold
Forced me to watch
The big lie unfold
I must now reveal
A tale so old
And told so often
It's covered in mold
My senior years
Are not gold!

Doris J. Chappius
Coeur D Alene, ID

Me, You and Us

Roses and violets are flowers
Cumulus and cirrus are clouds
Oceans and rivers are waters

Love, love and love is the
Universal language of those who care
About me or care about you

But merely rise like a flower
Move like a cloud, when
The sound of the wind,
Love spins like an ocean
Or runs like a river

Or merely care about me
Care about you, care
About us—care about
Flowers, waters, oceans
And clouds

Carmen I. Pierce
Danbury, NC

For Katie Reilly

Beauty incites a gaze
Trust endures
Timid murmurs
Defenseless haze

Shall I hunt or be hunted?
A recluse I'd be
Grasping a knee
Ere caution unwanted

As the eagle soars, so does my heart
Often fleeting
Sometimes bleeding
Comforted by beliefs of never being apart

Michael David Hinson
Myrtle Beach, SC

I Had a Dream

I had a dream
That my day was coming—
This year or next year,
It's gonna come.

I had a dream
That I was gonna make it;
No turning back now,
I must keep on.

I had a dream,
This was my dream.

I don't know what you've been told:
I had a dream
That I'll be brave, strong and bold.

Jesse James Badger
Yemassee, SC

Hesitant Company

You come and you go,
It isn't the first time your promises are left empty. . .
I never know if you'll stay.
Why am I surprised when you do?
Tears must be contagious—
They begin to stream down your cheeks,
Committing them to roll down mine.
Your words crack when spoken, you must be upset.
I want to believe that you're sorry,
Although I would just be lying to myself.
You beg for my company, and I hesitantly comply.
In the end, though,
No matter how happy we were in one another's presence,
You abandon me once more.
I must be naïve,
Maybe even dumb for letting you back in.
How can I say no to you? I love you, Daddy.

Naomi Goss
West Valley City, UT

Maturity

There's a time to stand
and a reason to fall
Understanding the silence
and knowing when to call

Our learned experiences
help balance the scales
Such journeys of grandeur
big words of tall tales

Recognizing opening and closing doors
some chosen, others left behind
We must make best of all things
attitudes positive, and emotions kind

We reap what we sow
discernment helps to know
when to stay or when to go
remain in servanthood, staying low

Jan Wallisa
Sullivan, IN

My Good Girl, Nola

My loving girl, Nola,
with a twinkle in your eyes,
you came to say goodbye.

You looked up at me
with your big, black, white-lighted eyes—
happy and relieved to be held
and boosted into bed and sleep.
Quietly suffering, such a lovely love as you.
You were a good girl, Nola,
special as can be.
Forever loved. Forever gone. . .
forever a beautiful memory
in my mind of my days gone.

Something special, I had—
My good girl, Nola, went home.

Susan D. Gorke
Venetia, PA

I See It Clearly

Did you hear? Did you see?
That ghostly figure
No sound, abounds
White as snow
Someone is looking—who can it be?

Haunting yellow piercing eyes
Nothing moves
No sounds I hear
Listen, the ghostly figure cries.

Do you see the glistening snow?
I see nothing, nothing at all
Wait, I see those eyes staring at me
They are high, I am low.

Woo, oh who could it be?
Who is that staring at me?
I wonder...

What does he see in me?
This bird of prey, talons large
He turns his head, the world to see,
This regal Snowy Owl.

Melissa A. Smith
Post Falls, ID

It is an honor to be recognized for my poetry. It has been a lifelong hobby of mine, and it seems to give me solace in the toughest of times. At a young age, I started to lose my sight and feel I must put my words down before I no longer could see them.

The Door

My life is a revolving door
People come, and they go.
Why and how they touch my life
Is not for me to know.
I stop to marvel why it is
A piece of some remain—
To mold me into what I am
Then rest in my domain.

Karen Odom
West Monroe, LA

*Examination of the great complexity of relationships inspired my poem.
People who nurture, who mistreat, who inspire, all have their place in my
life. Those people you admire for their strength, courage and faith never
leave you. There are those who believe in you more than you believe in
yourself. Such is the case of my much beloved sister, Jody Herren, who
initially submitted my poem.*

A Miracle Awaiting

Deep in the ground, and about to drown
From the loneliness that has come over.
There's no one here to save me
from what I'm going to be.
Dead and alone. .but now it is time to go
from this place so low—
and go lower and lower
To a place no one would ever want to go.
There is no hope, there is no life left inside of me.
I must go there; I'm so full of despair!
My life is ruined, and it can never get fixed.
As I'm finishing my journey,
I thought I'd never be free.
I'm finally there, and I'm choked with lava,
Now dead and alone. .dead and alone!
For there is no one here to ever save me.
My life is so full of secrecy—
Does Heaven even exist in me?
No! No! No!
Now, I meet the devil himself—
red and monstrous.
No wonder he must be the king of Hell.
Just before he touches me, a light shines;
it fills up the world, and an angel comes down.
She says to me: "Child, why are you here?"
I could not speak.
"Come with me, child; you will never be here."
The devil was in shock, and so was I;
an angel has never come down here before.
"This is a terrible place you do not need."
She takes me by the arm and lifts me free.
Now, I have beautiful wings and a magnificent dress—
I'm now an angel, and we fly to Heaven. . .
my new home!

Abby Payne
Salem, MO

She Still Stands There

She still stands there
Both tall and strong
She has faced
Her storm of life
The rain
The wind
While others have given in
Broken down by nature
She still stands there
Like a solider
She is a fighter
She stands there tall for all nations to see
She had her share of obstacles and woes
But she still stands there
She is fighter
She made it through her storm
And she's still there
For her country to see
Like her, I made it through my obstacles
Like her, it made me stronger
Into the woman I'm becoming

Juliana Asabea Amo
Philadelphia, PA

Immortality

These are the pros of immortality
There's been a thousand yous
There's only been one me
From the times of Columbus
To the dawn of history
I've seen the Panama Canal
And the splendor of Mt. Fuji
I've been to every country
Seen every type of human being
If you could only know
The things that I have seen
I helped build the Eiffel Tower
And rode the first boat
I was even present when they first discovered gold
I've lived forever
and others are dead
I won't say it again
It's already been said
You can't kill me
I'm already dead

Jeremiah Scott Burton
Waynesville, MO

The Earth Shook

The earth shook
Buildings fell
The people asked,
"Is this hell?"

The earth shook
Haitians died
People in shock
The whole world wide

The earth shook
People fled
No one knows yet
How many dead

The earth shook
So many lost
We must rebuild
At any cost

Donations coming
From far and wide
No helping hand
Will be turned aside

The earth shook
Haitians died
The earth shook
And the whole world cried

Elaine Cross
S Portland, ME

Untitled

Mountains breathing freshness
A newly fallen snow
Pines dispense an essence
Of warmth and soft pillows
Coffee sipped by fireside
Our gaze, the distant tide
Where earth and sky blend into one
Our day so rich has just begun
We meander along mountainside
Where elk and mule deer roam
We stop to stare as we see them graze
For this to them is home
In paradise, moose and mountain lion
So solitary now
Will befriend mankind and animals
Jehovah God knows how
We do thank Jehovah for His gift
Life we see all around
Life pulses with creatures, great and small
Vibrating with their sound

Delilah Koss
Lindsborg, KS

Oak Tree

I stand tall like an oak tree, sturdy and strong,
Or so it seems—to everyone but me.
What everyone sees is oh, so very wrong;
I am not strong and tall like the oak tree.
I really stand hurt and weak like a sapling:
Tired of the fight,
Weak from pain, and hurt from life.
One day, someone may see
That I am not the strong oak tree. . .
And maybe they will help me.
Until then, right here I will be—
The small sapling,
Pretending to be the tall, strong oak tree.

Malainee Renee Hilsabeck
Barnard, MO

The inspiration for this poem came from the loss of my grandfather. I was very close to him—my whole family was. When he took his life after battling lung cancer, we all took it hard. We all kept to ourselves, instead of going through the loss together. "Oak Tree" is a mix of how I felt through that time. Now, my family is back to normal. We still miss Grandpa dearly and are learning to move on, while keeping him with us. We will forever love you, Grandpa Eddie.

The Hook

The hook fastens your memories to the tree
And it holds them tight for all to see

The ornaments, either new or old
Tell the story of how our lives unfold

As our memories hang there twinkling in the light
It's the hook that keeps them hanging just right

So as you place your memories on the tree this year
Remember a friend who is always near

The hook, you see, won't let you down
They are very valuable and won't make a sound

So keep the hook as a treasure to you
'Cause, it will hold all that makes you, you!

Mikki Chavez
Tijeras, NM

No Longer There

Rain, rain,
Hitting my windowpane,
Keeping me inside for the day. . .
The comforting sound,
The crisp smell in the air.
Rain, rain,
Hitting my windowpane,
My sadness poured down.
Your presence is near;
I can feel you, but I can't hear.
Rain, rain,
Hitting my windowpane,
The darkness reminds me
I'm alone.
Thunder and lightning forming,
I was told it was just you bowling. . .
To give me some safety, some security.
You're gone, but it's still hard to believe.
Rain, rain,
Hitting my window. .pain.
Flashes, bringing me back to reality—
You're gone, no longer here with me.

Lauren Brown
Battle Creek, MI

Diamonds in the Grass

I see the tiny drops of dew
as a new day comes to pass
reflecting in the warm sunlight like
diamonds in the grass.

I seek for hidden treasures in the
darkness of the night—
a cricket's song, a star spayed sky,
a full moon's silvery light.

These are hidden riches in secret
places set apart,
and the only way to find them is to
search with all your heart.

Hidden blessings in each trial
when faith's put to the test:
to let us know that all is well,
and we are truly blessed.

Hidden lessons in the hard times
that always come to pass. . .
May we learn to look upon them
as diamonds in the grass.

Florence Grantland
Cherryville, NC

One More Day with Jack

Our task in life is not to reason
why we should live or die.
Jack and I took a walk to discuss
the important parts of our lives;
Jack and I shared our views of life.
I told Jack how it is important
to be a man and to stand up
for what you believe.
Jack had such a wonderful love,
trust and compassion
for each individual.
Like a plant or flower, we need
to have time to grow into
the beautiful people who we can be.

Keith Barringer
Saukville, WI

A Special Place

Meet me at a place, a special place
where laughter is heard.
Darling, I want to see your lovely face—
not another word.
Bittersweet memories shall be made
on the sunny shores;
Petty troubles of life, they will fade
to love forevermore.

Hear the sound of waves crashing,
the sound of couples laughing
as the tide tickles at their toes.
Listen to the seagulls yell,
ocean sounds in a conch shell
as a light breeze begins to blow.

Feel the sun beaming on your skin,
the salty water trickling in
as you strike a model pose.
Hold me close as the shutter clicks—
our sweet love, like in summer flicks,
as you fondly kiss my nose.

Kristina M. Peay
Columbus, GA

Family Christmas

'Tis the season to be jolly,
Saint Nick is on his way.
It's time for folks to gather,
and be merry on this day.

Our house will ring in laughter,
with the sound of children's glee
And eyes that gaze in wonder,
at the treasures 'neath the tree.

As we count among our blessings,
those things we hold so dear,
the most cherished of these moments,
is the love that lingers here.

All these pleasures that await us
will soon be ours to share—
We'll sing the songs of Christmas,
And be with ones we care.

Ron Hull
Laughlin, NV

Shrilling Cries

Christmas was just eleven days away,
everybody was excited.
The school was full of laugher and cheer.
Suddenly, unfamiliar noise caused anxiety.
Fearful teachers calmly tried to protect and shelter
their small students from harm and evil.

Suddenly, loud, shrilling cries all over
with pain and sorrow in Sandy Hook School.
'Twas around 9:38 AM on Friday, December 14, 2012
Twenty precious children's spirits traveled into Heaven.
Heaven's golden gate opened for intelligence and courage:
five adult heroic spirits filled the air
to help guide the young ones.

The twenty-six new spirits will be spending Christmas in God's house.
Their Savior Jesus, called the new ones by their names.
Jesus opened his arms—in that moment, such joy in Heaven.
Soft voices ask, "Where are our families? My Mom? My Dad?"
Jesus whispered to them, "I'll take care of your families."
Jesus looked down on earth saw so much sorrow;
He closed His eyes, stretched out His hands, and softly said,
"Let the presence of My power protect planet earth."

Betty Ruth Tollefson
Bagley, MN

The Sandy Hook school murders reminded me of the incident that happened in Hoy City, Vietnam. Many children the same age were murdered. The only difference was the adults were nuns, not educational instructors. I am originally from Fillmore, MO. I was raised on a farm, and my family had livestock and row cropped. I graduated in 1966 from Fillmore C-1 school and went to the school of nursing in Hinsdale, IL. I was also a volunteer nurse in Vietnam. I have four children, and my second marriage gave me three stepchildren. My husband and I are retired and live in Bagley, MN.

It's Days Like These

When I think of you
On a day just like today—
When the sky is blue and world is gay.
Lovers, hand in hand, walking in the park,
And I hear the song of a sweet meadow lark.
It's days like these, I swear,
I miss you most.

When I think of you
On a day just like today,
When the air is crisp and the sky is gray,
As I watch the leaves come tumbling down
And see hayrack rides all through the town,
It's days like these, I swear,
I miss you most.

For there's never been a single day
I didn't wake and call your name.
Searching for your face in every crowd,
Only to find you're not around—
You're still not around.

When I think of you
On a day just like today,
When the world is dressed in icy lace,
When the snow lies deep, and the earth lies still,
That's when I know—and I always will—
Every day of my life, I swear,
I'll miss you most.

Linn Ann Huntington
Hays, KS

Do You?

Sometimes, I just want to break a window
And scatter the shards from a mountaintop,
Or roll down a hill—tumbling, whirling, spinning—
Until breathing is an
impossibility.
Sometimes, I wish for purpose beyond
Teeth-brushing, education, social interactions,
Schedules.
Sometimes, I think it would be a relief
To be turned out into the vast world,
Uncertain and tender...drifting, but free.
Sometimes, it all becomes too much, and
I curl into myself while life spins on unperturbed,
And faces pass without emotion,
And the longing to be acknowledged, recognized, validated
Runs exquisitely deep.
Sometimes, earth and turbulent wind call to me,
Catch me unguarded—awaken the wild life-force within,
Beating her fists to burst out.
Sometimes, I want to put it all out there
Exactly as it is—raging, cosmic
Fire of the soul.

Claire McCulley
Niskayuna, NY

Villanelle

Sifting through leavings of another ago,
Old memories rise, and worries abound.
Love urges our hastening, but does it show?

Years of collecting must be faced as we grow,
Combining two houses in one go-around,
Sifting through leavings of another ago.

What shall we retain and what more shall we throw?
These books, this crystal, this linen, that mound. . .
Love urges our hastening, but does it know?

This ring. .a.new ring is needed; that, I know!
Yes, and a license! More chores for in town.
Sifting through leavings of another ago.

When off to a wedding, one never goes slow,
And struggling to get heavy things off the ground!
Love urges our hastening, but does it glow?

From the then to the now, we pitch to and fro
With head above flood; our resolve hasn't drowned!
Sifting through leavings of another ago,
Love urges our hastening—but does it grow?

Richard G. S. Finch
Medford, OR

My Land

There is a blue sky far above
Below is the land made for love
Oceans, deep blue and wide
Islands laying, side-by-side

Then lands of cotton, corn and hay
The land where man works every day
He builds a home, mighty and strong
He hopes to live there very long

The mountains reaching to the sky
All covered with trees, standing high
The meadows green, the valleys brown
As the sun sets, there is not a sound

Insects small, but really big
Tree held high, with just a twig
Man standing mighty on the sod
All of these were made by God

Shirley Ann Menefee
Sugar Creek, MO

The Game of Life

I looked down and saw how weary you came to be;
I reached down and took you to Heaven with Me.
We have the best seats in the house, and they're free.
If you don't like the score, I can change it, you see?
I am only here to make you happy—
Your mom's always worried about you, you see?
So I am the umpire now, and you're home free;
There's a game every day, and they tell Me, you see,
You're the best batter there is. .and I need you with me.
Mom and Dad, don't worry about me;
I have the best coach now, you see?
I'll watch over you now,
As you have always done for me!

Brenda A. Bub
St. Francis, WI

Too Old to Cry

Tell me: Are we ever
Too old to cry?
Although we face the world
And pretend that we *never*,
Tell me—are we *ever*
Too old to cry?

When we are young
The tears, they flow
Like vintage wine;
But as we older grow,
We try to stem the flow.
Tell me: Are we ever
Too old to cry?

Rose Burnham
Hayden, ID

My Beloved Twin

The days go by
So quick and fast
But the feeling of seeing you
Will never last
Since you been taken away from me
I have tried to come to peace
But every holiday and birthday
Fills my heart with our memories
It's hard to let go of you
My twin sister, it's true
You were my best friend
And I know I'll never find you again
I know you're in a better place
That's what people say
If they only knew you
Like I knew you
I think they would have wanted you to stay
Missing you, my beloved twin
I promise to love you
And try not to let the devil win

Shawna Bittle
Hope, AR

This poem was an opportunity for me to let everyone know how I feel inside due to my twin sister's death. My twin sister, Heather Kay, was taken from our family in 2006. It's a very hard thing to come to terms with; and even today, I struggle. Being a twin is a very unique gift to have, and to have someone take that gift...it's very hard to accept and overcome. Over the years, it's gotten easier; however, it still hurts. I do feel like she's still with me and my family, even though she's not here.

Distant, Fleeting Love

On wings of an eagle
you fly in with the wind
bringing me smiles
from faraway miles

Treasured moments together
happy then strained
for I know you'll be leaving
and life won't hold the same

As you ride the great eagle
to a land so distant and strange
I'm left behind
hoping this time
it won't be so long

Till my heart sings
its song
waiting for your return

Arleen Welch
Jacksonville, FL

Genealogy

God recreated His image when He made man
He gave him a garden, and all the land
Dominion was over all the living on earth
All of creation could create a new birth

Out of Adam, God made Him a mate
Woman, she is called to this very date
One flesh they would be, all their life
Today, we call them husband and wife

Adam named his wife Eve, meaning "life's giving"
Together they would be, to do their living
The serpent deceived Eve, which started sin
So penalties occurred for all women and men

Sorrow in childbirth would be the woman's fate
All because of the forbidden fruit that she ate
Cursed was the ground that Adam would till
Thorns and thistles, he would sweat for a meal

Wickedness became great, so man must die
Destroy the earth, came words from on high
Noah walked with God and found his grace
He would do God's will, whatever the case

Born of a virgin, Jesus was now here
People will praise Him, from far and near
The Savior had come to save gentiles and Jews
For many who believed, it was great news

Buddy Layman
Sardinia, OH

Christmastime in Colorado

When its Christmastime in Colorado,
  The ground is purest white.
The birds sing, the coyotes howl, the deer
  prance around. . .
I tell you, folks, it is a sight
  when snow is on the ground.

When its Christmastime in Colorado,
  All the world is in rejoice—
Just to sit by a blazing fire,
  And to hear each other's voice.
When Christmas time is over. . .
  Oh, to settle down to plan,
To plan the Christmas following, and
  To have it just as grand.

When it's Christmastime in Colorado,
  Then the snow is deep and wet.
When it's Christmastime in Colorado,
  That's a time you won't forget.

Mary Lou Stammler
Boulder, CO

The Shadow and the Voice

Crashing against my brain like a fearsome wave,
Pulling me in the dark abyss of a chilling reality cave.

Dashing and drowning,
Darkness surrounding.

Living for moments of the peaceful meadow,
Sleeping and hiding from my own shadow.

That dreadful thing,
Always reminding me
Of the way things used to be,
Before my brain surgery.

"Living for gaps between abyss and wave
is not the reason for the life that I gave."
This voice I hear is still, and I hear it travel—
Walking upon the sea as if it was thick gravel.

"Be still,"
The voice announces to the wicked water.
Then it holds me tenderly,
Just like a father.

Ashley L. Miranda
Tuttle, OK

Sunflowers, Sad Hours

Sunny faces, once bright and smiling into the sun,
bend over to stare at the ground—unable to hold up their heads.

Seeds drop like tears into the garden...too late to bring life,
sorrowful for the season's end.

Petals fall as promises do, soon to be forgotten.
Beautiful, green and hopeful now dried, brown and faded. .as love lost.

Tina Trujillo
Taos, NM

My love and I once grew beautiful, giant sunflowers in our garden. Then, one day, I believed it would all end. I looked out of the window at our flowers, and this poem was inspired. Happily, our love was renewed, and now we live on a sunflower-bordered lane that makes us smile as the years go by. I am a mother of four and a graduate of the University of New Mexico. My husband Andres and I reside in Taos, NM.

Potential

There is something that lies in our wake,
Something so much more than most realize,
Willing and capable to become known to all who are unaware.
Do you see the beauty that lies before your eyes,
Or, are you blinded by fate?

I can hardly fathom the chaos that will arise
When we open our eyes to our true potential.

Restlessly waiting deep in our souls,
Linked to one another, waiting to be set free from here—
We could, and very much will become whole again.

Watch me when I rise among you,
And do not be afraid of standing with me;
We must resist the curious, deceiving truth.

The outcomes are infinite, yet we choose our very paths.
I have taken mine, without a doubt.

I do not fail to refuse Fate.
I have come to realize that Fate is a tangible being,
Her thoughts and desires are not set in stone.

Allowing myself to watch the reality of this place in awe,
I am destroying our love for tainted desire. . .
Piece by piece, and moment by moment.

Rebecca McPherson
Kaufman, TX

Ode to My Friend

To Mary Ruth and Tom, this beautiful baby came—
The third one added to their picture frame.
A free-wheeling spirit along with his brother. . .
They would cover all territory, one way or the other.
As they grew up, many things would disappear
To be used on a project, where there was no fear.
Hitching a wagon to a calf in which they could ride. . .
Ended up in a fence, but it didn't kill their pride.
The animals got bigger and their ideas did, too;
There was no restraint in the minds of these two.
They tackled the world on top of rank bulls—
The outcome depended on which one they pulled.
Only the Lord could render a title like this...
Finally, "Rookie of the Year" in 1965.
The years have left his body with scars,
But his mind is capable of making him a star.
Writing poems, songs and books to fill his imagination,
Those talented words have made great creations.
He has a heart filled with compassion and love,
And he'll go to Heaven on the wings of a dove.
He has Jesus as his Savior until his life does end,
And I'm so proud to call him my dear friend.
No one's boots could fill a title like this—
Except my cowboy friend, Dan Willis.

Betty Hodde Hubbard
Robinson, TX

Seventieth Birthday

I never think of you as "old,"
No matter what we do!
You're always in there pitching
You always see it through. . .

I always think of you as "there,"
Steady, sparkling...eyes that care.
Handsome ways that make me proud;
Head on straight, not in the clouds.

I often think of you as "young."
You're quick to catch on. .and lots of fun.
Who would have thought when I took the job that day
We'd grow to love each other this way!

I often think of you as "smart,"
Discerning people from the start;
Measuring things to protect your own,
Trying to guide us steadily home.

I often think of you as "Dad,"
Having more children than you thought you'd have.
Helping them all to stay on the path,
Loving them always—imagine that!

Now, I see you as "Grandpa," too. . .
Surprising, how those children have influenced you!
"Grandpa, Grandpa!" Madi calls,
Even when you're not home at all.

I'm proud to think of you as seventy!
Eighty and ninety now have some levity.

Judy Seydel
LaGrande, OR

Child Eyes

The excitement that I had
Among the years of being young
It did not fade like a fad
But rather made me do all I've done

I've walked through the lava
Of red tile floor
And swam through oceans of bathtub
Where there were sharks galore

I battled the evils of fear
And held the world in my hand
That's right—the whole earth here
On a bouncy ball that sits on my nightstand

I finished my day drinking an elixir
That would make a mere mortal die
But you can drink if you know the trick, sir
It's called red and blue food dye

Oh, all these amazing things I've seen
And things yet to be done
Does it not seem so serene
In those child eyes of the young?

Ryan Maroni
Prescott Valley, AZ

Christmas

Christians praising
Happy songs
Reindeer flying
Inside and out, the house is decked out
Salt on the roads
Trees in the windows
"Merry Christmas" can be heard
Angels singing
Snowball fights are lots of fun

Joseph Carvell
Pulaski, TN

Annabella

When Annabella came into my life,
it was love at first sight.

As time went on, she grew up fast;
from day one, it has been a blast.

She cuddles when it is time to sleep—
but when it is time to play, she can play all day.

Jenny Goodwin
Monticello, MN

This poem was written to show the love between my cat Annabella and her cat parent, me. Annabella came into my life as a kitten and has now grown into an adult cat. Every day is different from the day before and is an adventure. Annabella has inspired me to look to the future of helping cats; but as of now, that is sadly still in the future.

Untitled

I think that time will never be
When seeds of Heritage we no longer see—
From the mighty winds that forever blow
To the four corners of the earth we proudly sow.

With God as our partner and Heaven our goal
We constantly seek refuge for our weary souls.
Let's seek to cross that great divide
And live forever in His abide.

Let not riches or goals or hidden treasures untold
Be the gap that separates His promises foretold.
With love for another to bridge that great tide
We shall safely cross to the Eternal side.

The sowers of seeds are you and me
They are scattered abroad by wind and sea
To every corner on this great earth
Foundations are laid, beginning at birth.

Gene Lackey
Gatesville, TX

In 1976, a Lackey family reunion was coming up, and my dad asked me if I had anything to contribute. I was driving on interstate 5 in Anaheim, CA in my work truck, and the words came pouring out. I wrote them down as I was driving.

My Special, Little Buddy

You came into my life as a baby, but at the age of two,
we became buddies—me and you.
We have shared the good,
And we have shared the bad;
But you will always be a fine, young lad.
Now the day has come to part,
But just remember: you have my heart.
I wish you well in all you do,
Because I will always love you.
You will always be my little buddy
Who could make my worst day like a beautiful blue sky.
You could and would be that special, little guy.
Just remember one thing before we part—
Your smile, hugs, kisses, and that little saying of yours
At naptime, "Goodnight, Miss Shirley, I love you"
Will always be a part of my heart.
You are and always will be my special, little buddy—
No matter where you are.

Shirley Stegall-Burgess
Burlington, NC

Where I'm From

I am from Hershey's kisses,
From Canada Dry Ginger Ale and Highland Chocolate milk.
I am from the smell of good cooking,
Delicious and amazing when it melts in my mouth.
I am from the willow tree,
The roses as delicate as they are beautiful.
I'm from pickles on the Christmas tree and humor—
From Jim, Kathy, and Elise.
I'm from the Wheel of Fortune after school and Sunday chicken,
From "Choose wisely and treat kindly,
and you reap what you sow" philosophy.
I am from the Cross over my door,
how it wards off evil spirits.
I'm from German, Scottish, and all my other parts,
From turkey and pumpkin pie.
From lessons of life you have given me. . .
The green eyes you have, and how they glimmer.
The hallway and library, where family pictures are hung in the
shimmering moon
and glistening sunshine of Arkansas for all to see.

Chris Remerscheid
Fort Smith, AR

Boots

Eight weeks old, full of vim;
Shelter life for pups is dim.

Part Black Lab, part Basenji:
"Take me, take me" was her plea!

Home she went, new Mom and Dad.
A brand new puppy. .Oh, egad!

Ate Dad's belt and credit card,
Always had to be on guard.

Mom took her for a walk each day,
Had many friends along the way.

Suffered surgery, injuries of knee—
Forget the cost!   Heal her, please!

Reciprocal love for eight-and-a-half years;
Then, what we learned brought forth the tears.

Tests confirmed the worst possible news:
Aggressive tumor, her life she would lose.

Symptoms worsened, we watched in despair—
How could we lose a companion so rare?

May of 2012, she took her last ride;
Mom crawled in the back to lie by her side.

Stopped for goodbyes with friends on the way,
Hugged us—not much anyone could say!

She rode on the stretcher to the caregiver vet. . .
A sedative first for our courageous pet.

The final assault, no longer in pain—
Our earthly loss is now Heaven's gain!

Esther M. Cantua
Lake Havasu City, AZ

Esther M. Cantua (*continued*)

My husband and I moved from New Hampshire to Arizona in 2002 to enjoy a temperate climate. Since our family was scattered around the country, we decided we needed a surrogate child. This entity would be an energetic, lovable puppy. We visited the local shelter and were smitten by this little eight-week-old. Boots was to become an integral part of our lives, becoming indispensable as she matured. Poetry has always been a catharsis for me. This poem helped me to process the grief felt during the time of her illness and subsequent passing.

Who Are You?

Who are you? One wonders.
Born in a world of sin,
not knowing who you are,
or what you are. . .
just what you've been taught
through the years.
Living beneath your greatest
knowledge and privilege,
not knowing who you are. . .
Never once considering that
Jesus is the best friend one can ever have.
This world is fleeting away fast,
we must find out who we are in time—
For one day, it won't matter who you are.
We were born to exist for a while,
to do a good deed and then travel on.
Travel where? To a new home
not made by man's hand.
There, no one will ask you who you are,
for it's there we already belonged.

Janice Prattis
Cambridge, MD

The Letter

I wrote the letter
Just to say, "goodbye"
I wrote the letter
I truly don't know why
I wrote the letter
When I was down and blue
I wrote the letter
So I could explain to you
I wrote the letter
When I felt all hope was lost
I wrote the letter
Not knowing what the cost
I wrote the letter
I wanted God to take us home
I wrote the letter
Because I felt so all alone
I wrote the letter
But I am sorry now
I wrote the letter
I will go on, somehow

Rose Linton
Pasadena, MD

You Can

In honor of Steven Souders (1963–1994)

Try not to stress when life gets tough
And the road is not so clear.
Keep your head held way up high,
And think of good and cheer.
Laugh a little, smile a lot—
You are in charge of you.
You are the best source that you've got,
What on earth is there to lose?
If you try and start to fail,
Don't ever lose your goal.
Remember there is always hope,
Deep down within your soul!

Angela Souders
Belton, MO

A Child's Death

I know it's not something we
Want to talk about,
But really, doesn't it make you
Want to scream and shout?

My friends have recently lost
Their twenty-year-old son.
He was their only child—
He was their only one.

I can't imagine their pain
Or the heartache that they feel.
I can only hope and pray
Through God's grace they will heal.

That as each day goes by
They continue to be strong,
And that through Jesus our
Saviour, they can live long.

Give up your thoughts and
Prayers for the lost young—
And hope and pray that
To our Saviour, they will come.

James A. Nelson
Aurora, NE

The Week Before. . .

'Tis the week before Christmas, and what's there to do
I've done all my shopping, I'm glad to be through

The Christmas tree stands in the corner, all green
It's glad to be there; it loves to be seen

Packages are wrapped in bright, cheery colors
A few for myself, and some marked for others

I'll go to the mall and watch people shop
Hurry here, hurry there...just shop till they drop

Not so for me, I've been down that road
I've looked and I've bought, and come home with a load

Make a trip to the kitchen, bake something sweet
On second thought, forget it—let's go out to eat

When Christmas is over and routine back again
Remember this week and how relaxed it has been

I'll take it in stride and try to remember
Shop early and often...and start in September

Enjoy the holidays filled with good cheer
Remember your blessings, and have a...

Happy New Year!

Joan Johnson
Brownwood, TX

River Beauty

As I looked upon the beauty of the river
Standing in it, staring out, I thought to myself
"I'm looking at God's tears."
The beauty of the clear water
Paralyzes the human body
While the sound gives the mind relaxation
That only God will give entrance.
The reflection of the wilderness
From the water nearly puts
Tears in my eyes
Tears not of sadness, nor of happiness
But of awe.

Josiah Metz
Iola, WI

Geometric Issues

Thirty, sixty, ninety
Which will it be?
Isosceles, equilateral
Too difficult for me.

Obtuse, acute
They all look the same
So why are they different
Each one, its own name?

Mary Ellen McPherson
Augusta, ME

Thoughts of Her

There's very few things that I have done lately,
The most time-consuming, thinking of my lady.
Thinking of her smile, her smell, her skin...
Wondering when I'll see her again.
I hope that it's soon—sooner than later.
But it's hard to say, back as a parole violator.
'Cause I did things I said I'd never do again,
and I went back around all my old friends.
It's not their fault, I accept all the blame;
I just couldn't stay away from the game.
Now I have found the one I need,
And that old addiction I won't have to feed.
Now she is my drug of choice.
What I wouldn't give to just hear her voice.
Her sweet smile—my girl, my baby,
These are the thoughts of her I've had lately.

Schuyler Danner
Pampa, TX

I have a beautiful family; a lot of the time, my family members are inspirations for my poetry. My Lord and Savior is the biggest inspiration, because nothing I do could be done without Him. This particular poem is about a friend of mine named K'Leigh. She, too, is a big inspiration for a lot of my poems. Thank you for taking the time to read this. God bless.

Proud to Be an American

A young boy was walking home
On the dusty road; he was all alone.
Talking to himself, he said aloud,
"I'm an American, but why should I be proud?"
An old woman from a house nearby
Heard these words and almost cried.
"Boy," she said, "come sit by me.
Listen to my story then you'll see."
As he walked to her there was a look of alarm
When she rolled up her sleeve to show numbers on her arm.
She told him of death and terrible things,
Things that only war can bring.
"I'll never see anything like it again.
I lost all my family. I lost all my friends.
When the war ended, I was sixteen years old,
And "Go to America" was what I was told.
God sent me to a country so new,
Just so I could talk to you.
You'll never lose what I have lost;
You'll never see what war does cost.
I am proud, because I am now free—
We have freedom as far as the eye can see."
As he walked home that day, he stood out in the crowd,
Saying, "I'm an American. That is why I'm proud."

Beth Davis
Calhoun, GA

This poem was inspired by God. It's that simple. I have allowed Him to take control of my life and use my talent for His glory.

New Year Puzzle

The New Year is here
A time celebrated with cheer
Many people state their resolutions
Some state them as mere executions
Many families tend to start over and give
Some just strive to sleep, work, and live
The New Year is a time for meeting expectations
From many, all, or some occasions
2013 has many months, birthdays, days and weeks
365, until it reaches its peak
There is so much to do, and so much to see
I wonder which way it will go—or will it be free?
Many people will carry the load of everyday bustles
For people who strive to live for the hustles
The holidays make us feel so special
Just thinking of them is such a wrestle
Babies are being born all year long
They are so free, cuddly, pure and young
January to December comes so quick!
Even St. Nick doesn't have much time to fix nor pick
Time does fly, as if it had wings
Sometimes it seems you haven't done a thing
Daylight savings time brings changes to some
Sometimes cool, and sometimes warm
Some people spend the year without new friends
Before you know it, it's the end
Time to do it again!

Stella Thomas
Memphis, TN

Museum of Unwritten Poetry

One autumn, when walking the backstreets of a dream,
I came upon a gray, stone building surrounded by a stout, iron fence.
Above the entrance were these words
Museum of Unwritten Poetry.
My hand, placed on a gate, closed on nothing

Over the door, I saw these words, *Free Admission to Poets Only.*
I passed inside as if there were no doors, no walls.
Inside, I found shelves and shelves filled with unexpressed thoughts,
Unwritten phrases, all labeled by subject and origin.

Those originating from the mind were neatly bound and labeled
by subject and time.
Those originating from the heart were a jumble,
stuck together with tears of joy or pain.
The aisles were covered with used words that crackled underfoot
like autumn leaves.

The place seemed abandoned, but there was no smell
of dusty volumes or disuse.
Then, I noticed lines of people at the back door,
Hurrying forward like ants—dumping armloads of materials
and taking nothing in return.

Then watching further, I spied a trickle of people coming in the front door
To take poems from the shelves, gather bundles of words from the floor
And pass quietly out the door.

I too took as much as I could carry and left quietly.
As I walked away, I looked around,
And lo, the building was gone.

Fred L. Dayharsh
Spokane, WA

Struggle

I do not know your feelings,
And I don't know mine;
Therefore, I hide my pain and say I'm fine.
Being friends will work for now,
However, will it forever?
How long before I cave.

I picture us together,
You have hurt me twice, but I cannot let go;
despite my efforts the tears still flow.
Are you the person I know
Or now, are you someone I knew?
I begin to wonder if I ever really knew the real you.
All the late night talks,
All the shared secrets—

Were they real, or just a regret?
I cannot tell.
Therefore, the past I weep.
Sick to my stomach,
My body will not let me eat.
My simplest needs, I cannot meet.
My friends can only guess the pain I feel inside;
So I take my tears in and I make my heart hide.
You may never know how much of me is true,
But no matter your actions—
I still love you.

Stephanie Hoover
Grand Haven, MI

Simple Lies

See myself in others
But never in myself

See the pros and cons
But nothing truly defined

That I have to make
For what it is

Someone who is always
Forgoing transition

Are we ever truly
One defined?

Or only that which we make
Of ourselves from those around?

Positive or negative
Right or wrong

The eye of the beholder
Will never really decide

Cursed shadows
Show trials of those past

Allowing the options
To be ever-present

Yet, a new choice
Must be made

The wrong?
Perhaps

Only simple lies
To make old look anew

Jeffrey J. Michalowski
Allenton, WI

If There Was Any Justice

If there was any justice
in the world
my mom would understand
that being a kid
isn't always
perfect

If there was any justice
in the world
I would see my brother
every day, wake up
with him in the room
next to mine
being the big brother he is

If there was any justice
in the world
he would love me again
hold my hand
hug me tight
and be proud to say, "She's mine"

If there was any justice
in the world
people wouldn't judge others
some they hardly know
but judge anyways
just because
they don't act or look alike

Camryn Creedon
Britton, MI

My Heart's Delight

In the darkness of the night
I awaken

Inner light is calling, calling, calling
calling me, true
brighter than gold
more pervasive than air

Inner light
My heart's delight
breathe, breathe, breathe
slowly now, breathe

Inner light
soothes, rocks
holds, cradles and cuddles
no words, no lullaby

yet
softness and sound
Inner light
the presence so fair

Inner light
my heart's delight
Inner light
my best friend

Darlene E. Jolley
Bloomfield, IN

Once Upon a Christmas Wish

Once upon a Christmas rhyme,
A snowman paused bleak and wary,
Despairing o'er his brief time—
Yule's reason to be merry.
But no time to wish for more,
For too soon, he'd be nevermore.

Could he but begin again,
How many wishes he'd inspire. . .
Eyes and smile coaled in
And turned up carrot nose afire.
How young and old cheered for more
While playing at their happy chore!

Light came upon a midnight clear,
When an Eastern star shone most bright
And vanquished the snowman's fear
Of a life so short, but so right;
He'd come each year to restore
Man's Christmas spirit evermore!

Mark Gray
Aurora, CO

This Drug Called Love

The anticipation slowly builds with each passing moment
Like a forest fire spreading with the wind.
Its heat is rising, and I can feel the passion all around me.
Should I give into the lust as it entices me to come closer?
I feel pleasure with every step I take closer to the flame.
Mixed emotions of pain and desire enfold me in a blanket.
I have thirst that I can't seem to quench without getting closer.
I'm yearning for more. .one more step, and I'll get another fix.
This drug called love is too intense to confine.
And why would we?
A bird is most beautiful when it is free and wild;
In its astounding radiance, you will find something pure, something true.
To give in to it is to lose control—
It can end in glory, or it can end in darkness.
Is that a chance we're willing to take,
Or would we rather just behold it in all its majesty...
As something free, something wild, something pure, and something true...
And with that, let it go?

Dominique Martin
Fayetteville, NC

Nothing More Precious

There's nothing more precious than little boys and girls
Smiling, laughing and having fun in school
There's nothing more precious than parents
Teaching their children God's golden rules

God bless the children
God bless the families
God, pour out Your spirit, and help the parents go on
And the other children succeed in life

God, rain down joy on the children
God, bring peace to this cruel world
God, help the teachers
Whose little students' voices will no longer be heard

God, save America
God, save this Universe
Teach us to love one another
Teach us to love the state of Connecticut and the elementary school

Teresa Harrell Moten
Alexander City, AL

Symphonic Visions

Each day passes, and I stare into the eyes of the moon
She washes over me in sweet, silver showers
I chase the stars, capturing each bit of light within my fingertips
Each breath I take, making me see further
This kaleidoscope of color, burning and bursting before me
Picking at my skin like electricity
My mind, a new world of possibilities
My heart, in pure rapture

I feel the earth, soft beneath my bare feet
The whisper of the wind caressing my skin
Each memory of the trees
The great, wise willow stretching out to embrace me

I lift my arms in wonder to this dream that plays before me
I am floating, flowing like liquid
Each movement, like that of a butterfly's wings
A moment so great. .time forgotten

This scene like no other
No feeling so great
None as wondrous
As this sweet moment of peace set in my grasp
This enticing vision of magic and melody

As I lay here in this symphony of cosmic desire
In this beautiful lullaby of color and bliss
As we two dance
For one last moment in the end

Kelli Kathleen Atchley
Spiro, OK

Simply Love

Glance
Look
Eyes
Meet
Smile
Blush
Talk
Friendship
Coffee
Movie
Dinner
Lust
Touch
Love
Question
Yes
Together
Forever

Donna E. O'Neil
Franklin, TN

"Simply Love" was penned during a reflective moment. The poem showcases the excitement of a relationship at every level, taking twenty individual words and unifying them to embrace the dream of happily ever after. After a successful career as a newspaper reporter and editor in Massachusetts and Tennessee, Donna O'Neil is chasing her dream and pursuing a career as a fiction writer. Follow her on Twitter at "offdeadline."

The Last Time

I've walked this land
I've walked before
This one last time
There'll be no more

I walk the rooms in this old house
Where years of living now are past
You're gone, no more to be
And it will never be the same for me

When I drive down the lane one last time
I'll take the memories, for they are mine
To draw upon as I grow old
You're here no more for me to hold

Frankie Gotti
Minneapolis, KS

I am seventy-three years old, and my husband and I were both farmers and raised cattle for many years. This poem is what I wrote when I decided to leave our lifelong profession after my husband died. It doesn't describe exactly how I felt—there are really no words to describe that feeling.

The Senior Ball

It's half-past eight, and we can't be late;
We're going to a ball.

I told my mate we shouldn't be late. . .
But where it is, we can't recall.

Oh, what a fate! Neither myself nor Kate
Can remember the address of the hall.

Last year, maybe, it was a big estate—we remember a gate,
And inside was a long, brick wall.

Long tables, where we ate, and centerpieces that I hate
And a waiter that had a deep, southern drawl.

We got a call from Nate, "Look at last year's souvenir plate,"
He said: "It's at the Church of St. Paul."

We arrived in a state that one couldn't berate—
I in a tux, and Kate in long dress and a shawl.

We saw on the slate, the menu was au fait. . .
We found the servings much too small.

The music was great, those seniors danced with a special gait—
But Kate and I slept through it all.

Stanley T. Gray
Mountain Home, AR

Forever

Do not cry, My child
Your momma isn't coming home
I am forever with you
They call me your Heavenly Father
I am your Lord and Savior
Do not be afraid, My little child
I know all the abuse you've gone through
You don't know how to love me
I will forever love you
You can call My name
I am forever yours
I know you feel lonely, child
You have been searching for Me
And you do not understand
What are you searching for
Come with Me
Let Me be your world
Because, my child
I want you to return home
So I can forever stay with you
So you won't ever feel alone

Nikki Kennison
Pairesville, OH

Poetry of Love

No greater expression of love is found
Than in a poet's hallowed ground,
For in his poem of emotional toil,
Love springs eternal in fertile soil.

No mailed knight so rigorous sought
A quest as futile as a poet's thought.
Where the theme is love, a passionate heart,
Only a fruitful pen, a solitude of parts,

Can grant any soul its brief respite—
A brief flame in the absence of light,
Futile words that try to impart
Poetry of love from a wishful heart.

Joe Robert Surber
Claremore, OK

Tomorrow

Before I met you, each day drug by
Each sunrise I came to despise
Now, I see tomorrow in your eyes

My life was filled with drugs, booze and lies
No one gave a damn if I lived or died
Now, I see tomorrow in your eyes

A heart can be broken only so many times
It takes passion to live a life
Now it's time to open your eyes

Chad Jungers
Morton, IL

Mama

Mama was a special person
  dear to our heart
Her sacrificing love truly
  set her apart

Her hands became rough
  and worn
Because she worked so hard
  since all seven of us were born

We grew up very poor
  but rich we were
Because we had a kind, loving Daddy
  and a strong-willed mother like her

Mama always helped others
  in her neighborhood
By lending a helping hand
  and doing what she could

She supported her church with
  faithful attendance and love
Because she patterned her life
  after our Father above

Mama's earthly life is over
  but she now rests on that shore
Free of pain and suffering
  beyond Heaven's golden door

Carolyn Councilman
Graham, NC

Momma, She's Good Enough for Me

The time has come, dear Mom
To release your desire to control your son
Sixteen years of marriage only proves she's here to stay
Our wedlock is strong, as the *Bible* tells us a husband and wife become one

Manipulating, game-playing. . .
Did that get the result you wanted?
We'll need to have sustained trust-building
For healthy relations and get-togethers to happen

Sad we can't even talk any longer
Wonder how God will work this out
Our marriage and faith is strong
Jesus is the only answer

Be a part of the resolution you want to see
We'll be watching for change
Positive vibes in your life and communications
We love you and wish you everlasting joy!

Galen Herbic
Liberty, MO

Night Walk

Breathe honeysuckle,
Pet red fur.
Glow under the moon,
Love the night.

Breathe and grow. . .
Water and grow.
The moon is
A patient and subtle soul.

She makes you stand
Taller than you thought
And draws your shadow true.

Moonlight gives sparkle and strength
To the night world—
And to me.

Brittany Denbow
Thayer, MO

The Darkness Inside

The darkness inside rips you apart
it makes you see things that aren't here
So the darkness always knows where to start
When you have nightmares, it makes it stronger
Shadows surrounding you, suffocating you
you can't breath, you can't sleep
Everywhere you go, it's there
when you turn out the light
even when you die
But when darkness can overpower you
there is nothing you can do
Hell is consuming your body
you can't escape it
Darkness is in everyone
No matter where you go, it's there
it's the darkness inside

Jessica Jones
Good Year, AZ

The Chase

I watched the rabbit come over the hill;
he watched and waited, till all was still!
Then he hopped very slowly around a log—
he didn't know I had a dog.
All was still till the dog arose;
he sniffed the air and followed his nose
around where the bunny had last been seen.
His sense of smell was very keen!
The rabbit was hidden, or so he thought. . .
he hadn't counted on meeting Spot!
The rabbit took off in a zigzag run.
Spot took off, too—my, what fun.
He didn't catch him, the rabbit too wise. . .
ran into a hole that was just his size.
Spot dug a little and sniffed a lot.
His tongue hung out—boy, was he hot.
He came back to me, and we sat real still. . .
another rabbit came over the hill.

Edythe Morgan
Rollins, MT

God's Song

'Twas during a dreamful sleep a vision came to me,
From a past-life or a peculiar memory. . .
Inside a paradise I had never before seen,
Alabaster sands and waters shining blue-green.
An unfamiliar silence encompassed me,
Wildflower scents danced on the breeze—
Only, in the distance I did not expect to see
One Who would surpass all my needs.

I was intrigued by this Man leisurely sitting on the sand,
Who picked up and placed a cherry oak-colored violin in His hand.
Da, Da, De, Da, Da, Dum...the tune floated across the water as perfumed air;
His presence was ethereal, with talent beyond rare.
Seemingly unknowing of how captivated I would be,
He played to an audience of the wind and the sea.

With the clarity of crystal bells ringing in my mind,
I knew this Man was Jesus, Healer of the blind.
I seemed to float across the shore to the One in white;
The music halted, His peaceful demeanor stole my fright.
I looked at Him through eyes blurred with tears,
Wanting His song to cleanse me of wasted years. . .

When I awoke, the music still lingered in my head,
But I only noticed a cherry oak violin resting by my bed.
Through my window, a soft, summer wind blew.
The dream was real to me, I know God's love is true.
So during seasons of stormy and still, the ocean is a solace for me—
There, yet again, I hear God's song riding off the ripples
of the white-foamed sea.

Sarah Marsh
Millersburg, MI

Springtime in the Mountains

When it' springtime in the mountains
And the air's so fresh and new
All the flowers on the hillside
Takes in the morning dew

Now the petals on the roses
Ripple in the daytime breeze
And the sound of many songbirds
Can be heard among the trees

When the new born of creation
Frolic in the noonday sun
They jump and play most every day
'Cause their lives have just begun

Now life has many changes
And time will take its toll
But we never know where our lives will go
Or if we ever meet our goal

So when it's springtime in the mountains
When the air's so fresh and new
All the flowers on the hillside
Took in the morning dew

Samuel Bennett
Sturgis, SD

My Dream

Making changes,
Taking chances,
Curiosity over-raging!
Gazing at beauty unlike any other!
Watching as others get what I wish!

You shine like the ocean,
With the sunsets' reflection. . .
Pure beauty!

Standing still,
I look back now—
Every moment and dream is awakening!
Staring into passionate eyes,
Kissing on luscious and pure lips!
All I've ever wanted is this!

Happiness takes over,
Finally getting that chance!
Scared of losing
This romance!

Dakota Norman
Bedford, IN

The Inkless Pen

My clipboard awaits with paper and pen;
It beckons me near, a new poem to begin
As I search my imagination for a topic anew,
And toss around an idea or two.

Shall I create one that rhymes? I'll give it a shot.
Now, what was I thinking? Oh, darn, I forgot!
Try as I may, the words just won't come.
Is my brain in a coma? My "thinker" feels numb.

Is this what's referred to as "writers' block?"
I'm hopelessly distracted by the tick -tocking clock.

Well, tomorrow is a fresh, new day;
Perhaps a great subject will then come my way.
Meanwhile, I'll try to come up with an end
For this poem I can't write. . .
There's no ink in my pen!

Kathryn Buck
Yucca Valley, CA

The Elegance in a Butterfly's Wings

There's such beauty and elegance
in a butterfly's wings
as they float and flutter by;
they always catch your eyes.
They float and sway,
and seem to say:
"You're beautiful, too, in God's eyes!"
The elegance in a butterfly's wings...

Mary Deal
Sibley, LA

Conner

Curious, cute and cuddly, my grandson is to me
the only one—but so much fun—sitting on my knee.
New toys always amaze him, he studies them very well;
Now that he's two, the toy sounds he makes are truly really swell.
Everyone loves him dearly, he has a heart of gold. . .
Really extra-special, a joyous gift to behold.

Anne M. Sample
Scranton, PA

As an educator for thirty-one years, teaching first-graders made me look at the world through their eyes. Their excitement and enthusiasm about learning was a joyous occasion for me to witness. Now as I look at my grandson's learning process, I can again feel that same emotion I felt years ago as he explores the world. I also reflect upon that same experience I felt when my son was that age. I compare my son's and grandson's similarities and admire the characteristics Conner possesses that make him unique.

You Don't Know Me

There was kept a file upon a shelf
A reflection of yourself
In this file, there is a list
Not a prejudice is missed

From a mind that is so narrow
You can't pierce it with an arrow
Shoot you down, just like a sparrow

Judge you by first appearance
They won't give you any clearance
When they look to see your difference

A thief who died stole paradise
A heart of gold, his merchandise
When he spoke to the One Who Judas kissed
Is there something that we all missed?

Let the innocent cast the stone
We are guilty to the bone
Would be none but God alone

We must care for one another
Every one—your sister, brother
Any judgment is reserved
For the One the angels served

For anyone who cannot see
This one is for you and me
Because you really don't know me!

Kenneth Hinkle
Winchester, VA

The Waiting Place

Like a forest in the winter, with branches stripped and bare
looking lonely and neglected against the winter sky
they sit there in the winter of their life
in that waiting place to die

Oh, they call it a nursing home
but just between you and I
it's just a stop before the grave
this waiting place to die

Backs that were once strong and straight
feet that were swift and spry
now shuffle slowly down the hall
in that waiting place to die

They sit there lonely and wait
for a loved one to drop by
lonely for a voice, a touch
in that waiting place to die

When my time here is done
and the years have passed me by
I pray that God will let me miss
that waiting place to die

Galen Belcher
St. Joseph, MO

Another Hill to Climb

She went for her mammogram, as she does every year
The usual news was expected: everything's free and clear
But this year was different, and caution be heeded
They said, "Come back in, a biopsy is needed"

We made an appointment as soon as we could
When we got the news, the news wasn't good
We all know that cancer is a terrible disease
When they say, "you" have cancer, it makes you weak in the knees

We went to the doctor we wanted the best
She had the results of all of the tests
She spoke in a language that just doctors know
What I heard in the end was, both breasts have to go

My wife quipped as she does just to make me feel better
"Well, I won't look the same when I put on a sweater"
So I squeezed her hand in our own special way
And smiled, so she knew that I was okay

This all happened so fast, is this all really real?
Words can't express just how helpless I feel
But a man must be manly, and manly I try
When she can't see me is when I can cry

We have faced life together for forty-six years
There's been laugher and sorrow, and sometimes there's tears
We will face this together, though it will take time
Hand in hand, we will face it...one more hill we must climb

Bernard L. Thieben
Chillicothe, IL

My wife Beverly and I live near Peoria, IL along the Illinois River. I am retired. In 2009, my wife had a bilateral mastectomy operation. After her surgery, she was sent home to recover, and a visiting nurse was assigned to help with her recovery. The nurse said, "You have been through a traumatic experience, and it sometimes helps if you write about what you went through." Then she told me, "You went through this experience with her and should also write about your feelings." That's when I wrote "Another Hill to Climb." Beverly is now cancer-free.

Heart of Mine

Broken heart,
wondering if it is real.
I sit and think about
what my heart is
really going through,
all the things I go through
in life...I think about what
I'm going through tonight.
What kind of love is this?
To know it all starts with
someone being in my life,
then ends with
wants and wants. . .
and goes nowhere.

Evelyn Padilla
Lakewood, CO

Are You Ready for Christmas?

Are you ready for Christmas, are you making your plans?
Have you baked some yummy cookies? Do you have a dozen hands?
Are the stockings hung, the carols sung, the gifts under the tree?
Have you scheduled all the parties? Is there time for a cup of tea?
Are the cards and letters written to friends both far and near
To say how much you miss them and wish that they were here?

Has Santa packed his sleigh with toys? Oh, the presents he will bring!
The time is fast approaching; have you forgotten anything?
Of course, to the Christmas pageant at church or school to go:
The laughter, the music, the costumes, the fun—maybe it will snow!
Many things take up our time at this special time of year,
So why do we feel so empty when Christmas is almost here?

To really be ready for Christmas, your heart you must prepare
To welcome the Messiah—God's gift beyond compare.
A gift of the wonderful promise in Jesus Christ the King
Of hope and love and peace and joy, the salvation that He brings.
Focus on the spiritual as Christmas comes around;
Take time to feel God's presence, your soul with joy abounds.

And Christmas Eve will find you with all your errands done.
The time is nigh to hold Him dear—Christ Jesus, God's own son.
The ancient story comes to pass, the prophecy fulfilled:
A baby born in Bethlehem to save the world, God's will.
So as your Christmas plans unfold, remember just one thing—
The reason for the season is the birth of Christ, the King.

Robbie Heintzman
Prescott, AZ

Nothing Better

I think that possibly, maybe, I'm falling for you
Because I love the way his eyes sparkle when he smiles
How there was nothing better than the magic of his kiss

I think that possibly, maybe I'm falling for you
Because I love the way my hand fits perfectly into his
How we can laugh and joke for hours on end

I think that possibly, maybe, I'm falling for you
Because I love the way I feel when around you
How you're the only one I want to tell my secrets to

I think that possibly, maybe, I'm falling for you
Because some people refuse to settle
For anything less than butterflies

I think that possibly, maybe, I'm falling for you
Because there's nothing better than the moment
When you realize you're falling in love

Melissa L. Kunz
Canfield, OH

Stars and Stripes

Stars and stripes
red and blue
battle cries
fight for you
on the battle
all men fight
a long day
a restless night
fear of death
hide away
uncertainty
very afraid
tears of women
letters received
crying children
as families leave
joy turned to sorrow
sorrow made tears
tears to sorrowful screams
anger changes
anger flees
sympathy is all we need
when we lose someone
to the angry war
but peace redeemed
we fight no more

Michaela Carr
Jacksonville, IL

Daddy

Days of sadness still overcome me,
hidden tears so often flow;
memories keep you near me.
Although you died ten years ago,
there will always be a heartache
and, often, a silent tear.
I cherish those special memories
of days when you were here.
Remembering you is easy,
I do it every day.
Missing you is a heartache—
that never goes away.

Poet Johnson
Linton, IN

The Hard Woods

The woods contain thousands of trees, bushes, and ferns. . .
The deepest of nature is held hostage of hidden messages.
Raising three generations in these thick woods,
Grandpa reveals advice of eternal life.

Robin Conlon
Clintonville, WI

The Hunt

What hunt? Oh, the hunt,
It's neither the kill,
But the ecstasy of the mind.
With taught muscles of twisted steel,
And throbbing heart within the ears,
Keen of eye and nerves of voltage—
The forefinger, frozen upon the trigger.
There, there, the majestic animal comes,
Meandering in the serenity of the autumn morning. . .
Clear and crisp with the fragrance of the needle laden floor.
Now, the mind computes the deadly kill,
Flashes, wait—wait!
Look, look at that majestic animal standing,
Nostrils flared and breath vaporizing into the air. . .
Oh, the inebriation of a triumphant hunt.

William Irwin
Middletown, MD

The Gossip Shed—James 1:19

In the front yard at the site of the old home place
stands our favorite meeting place
My siblings and I nicknamed it the gossip shed...almost a gazebo style
With four open sides and mounted porch swings and a tin-metal roof
That is so inviting and so supreme.
It used to be my grandfather's outdoor water well shed
Until my father moved it and made it a unique outdoor gathering shed
My siblings and I often meet there to talk about social and personal events
Did you know I've been told that ninety percent of communication
Is done through hearing and not speaking!
Now I believe what the Holy Scripture says,
"To be slow to speak and swift to hear," James 1:19
That is why I believe God gave us two ears and only one tongue
We talk about our past memories, some good and some bad
I think about what the apostle Paul says in Philippians 3:13
about forgetting the past—
"I press forward to the high call of the Lord."
And, when our discussions lead to the present time,
I think about the Lord's prayer, "Give us this day our daily bread."
Read the rest of Jesus' prayer in Luke 11:24
And then, when the future plans are discussed,
the Holy Scripture comes to mind
James 4:14-15, "If it be the Lord's will, I will do that which I have spoken."
In summary, when I am tempted to gossip,
the old saying that my parents taught me...
"If you can't say something good about someone, don't say anything at all!"

Barbara S. Henson
Milner, GA

This short story or poem is based on a family tradition. There is an old childhood saying, "Sticks and stones may break my bones, but words will never hurt me." But, oh, can't they? Read this poem over and over again— the enlightened message can apply to all generations!

No Reason

Have you ever wanted to cry for no reason?
Just let the tears fall like your own season?
Not because you're in pain,
Or you're angry and have nothing to gain.
Not because you're happy or afraid,
Or even because you were played or betrayed.
But you lie there in bed,
You're eyes start to prick;
Breathing becomes a lie, and you're not even sick.
But the cost of life is high,
And all at once, you get your fill...
Then the water starts to spill.
Down your cheeks, the tears are round.
Head swirls for a reason, but there's none to be found.
So you cry for no reason. . .
and don't make a sound.

Marissa Brown
Mitchell, IN

Storm raging outside, I try to sleep. I live in Mitchell, IN, in the house I share with my parents and older brother. It was here my poem came to me. Like I said, a storm was raging outside as well as in my heart. I was conflicted and didn't know what to do, so I described the feeling in "No Reason." Every word is a picture of what I felt that storming, dark night. I am thirteen years old.

The Fly

You flew inside my classroom today,
And you quietly sat down, right in my way.
I tried so hard to read aloud the book,
But instead of me...only to you, they'd look.
"Now, boys and girls, pay no attention to that fly."
I began again...*swat!* You chose to die!

Greta Young Rowland
Dalton, GA

I have been teaching elementary school in my hometown for twenty-seven years now. I'm married to Brad, and we have three children: BJ, Ally, and Will. I love writing humorous poems about things that happen in my classroom and around my school. I'm called the "Cata Mom" in our community, because I'm such a big fan of my alma mater, the Dalton High School Catamounts. I love playing tennis and traveling to Jamaica every chance I get. I live by the philosophy, "Say what you mean, mean what you say, and do what you say you are going to do."

Old Bones

"Old Bones, It's alive! Run, Mema, run!" she screamed
As she flew out the door, hitting her pal Tom
So hard it sent him reeling.

"Babe, what in the world's a-happenin'?"
"Tom, Old Bones raised up, looked at me like I'm lunch."
"Old Bones, what's that?"
"You, go look—tell me."

Tom's quietly fighting fear, though soon forgotten
When he thinks of Babe seeing him a hero.
He gingerly climbs up to the window and peers in.
Suddenly, whooping laughter, over and over!

He sees she's angry and senses scratch city.
He comes over, puts his paw on hers and asks,
"Babe, Honey, would you like to go rat hunting?"
"Oh, Tom, my favorite sport. I guess he knows me better than. .".

He must face Babe and tell her Mema's malfunctioning
Hospital bed without a mattress Is Old Bones!
That impish shadow toyed with her mind. . .
He's afraid if she feels embarrassed, she'll take it out on him.

Thelma M. Hobart
Oklahoma City, OK

Compromise

I blame you, you blame me
Who's to say who is right or wrong?
I believe I am right
You believe I am wrong
You believe you are right
I believe you are wrong
Why can't we compromise?

There are so many reasons
I can offer to defend my beliefs
There are so many reasons
You can offer to defend your beliefs.
Who's to say I am right?
Who's to say you are right?
Why can't we compromise?

Where are our strong beliefs coming from?
Are they self-centered?
How will others benefit?
How will others suffer?
Consider the consequences
Take time to find solutions.
Why can't we compromise?

Gertrude Payton
Milwaukee, WI

Poetic words express concern of the poet as observed by the poet's actions towards individuals. There appears to be a society of people divided into two distinct categories: men and women who seemingly understand the importance of working together for the good of all, and men and women who seemingly are self-centered and less considerate of the consequences for others. It would be beneficial if both sides were to stop, think, and evaluate the total seriousness of the consequences. The poet is a retired educator and the author of a book, titled A Caregiver's Journey *(2009).*

The Time I Wrestled a Bear

While walking through the forest one day
In the merry, merry month of May,
It came to my surprise that I heard footsteps from behind.
I heard a tramp, I heard tromp, I heard a bump, bump, bump. . .
I heard a tramp, I heard tromp, I heard a bump, bump, bump.
I suddenly stopped, turned and saw a lump!
The lump continued to go bump, bump.
It rose, and I swear, it was one big bear!
It was the biggest bear I ever saw,
it was bigger than the one I saw in Arkansas!
I froze in terror and did not know what to do,
So I turned around, and I flew.
I ran real fast, but not fast enough;
The bear was quickly catching up.
I heard a bump, bump, bump.
The sound was getting nearer, and I thought I was out of luck.
Then it hit me—through the air I flew, and I landed with a clunk.
I started wrestling that bear.
He was large and brown and had a lot of hair.
He was big and he was strong, but he was also all brawn.
I pinched his nose, and he growled in pain;
I thought for a moment, "This is such a shame."
His poor, little nose turned bright, cherry red,
Then, he ran all the way back to his warm, cozy bed.
And that's the story of when I wrestled a bear.
This is not a lie, I swear.

Joseph Campion
Bethel Park, PA

He Does What's Best

As days go by without speaking your name,
I get worried and frightened of the good Lord's game.

Sometimes I sit and wonder why
He gave us this tragedy that caused a big cry.

Was it because we take life for granted,
Or forget where our roots are morally planted?

Did He do it to make us wake up,
To remind us to thank Him for the food on our plate
and the drink in our cup?

As days go by and I think about you,
Memories come to mind out of the blue.

I cherish these memories with all my heart,
And my understanding of God's game begins to start.

He takes every action for a reason.
He knows what's best for every occasion.

I'll never question God's decision again,
Because He's Who gave me memories with you
that will last until life's end.

Brittany Stallings
Kenbridge, VA

My poem is inspired by my grandmother. Today, she is a walking miracle after surviving several bleeds to the brain. Doubtful that I'd ever speak to her again, I turned the situation over to God. My faith in Him reached extremities I never knew it could reach. God turned my grandmother's life around and blessed me with her presence. If ever I had a doubt about God, my grandmother's survival altered my beliefs and revealed the true power of prayer.

Storm Fear

There's a storm on the horizon, predicted by the early-dark sky;
I'm not afraid, I've been through these things before.
No need to worry—
You're here with me, safe at home.

Thunder rumbles in the distance, growing louder and closer
Until it erupts into a deafening boom.
Zigzags of lightning perform an unwelcome light show
With too many encores.

Maybe I'm not scared, but our pets are.
The cat has scurried upstairs to her bunker under the bed.
Unlike his cat friend, the dog has no desire to go it alone;
He clings to us like a too-tight sweater.

Powerful wind-gusts bully trees into submission,
Limbs and branches bow low;
If they can't bend, they break.
Rain is much needed, but not this much. . .
This is more like a gigantic broken water-main.

Still, I'm not really terrified,
But—I did make us some tea, as if to ward off danger.
Silly, I know. I'll be so thankful when it's over. . .
Then, I'll remember it sure was frightening.

Shirley Cornelius
Kansas City, MO

Christmas Expectation

The kids were in anticipation over their Christmas expectation
The pile was less, a smaller accumulation caused by inflation
The parents were in sedation, not ready for the occasion's obligation
The kids wanted to peek and slit the paper, causing ventilation
A finger-made penetration—flipping a switch, causing sound and vibration
Oh, was it a cell phone or a game? It had no insulation
Such temptation at this time of huge expectation
They waited noisily for their parents to rise from hibernation
But finally decided to tickle their noses with a red carnation
Dad and Mom jumped up with sleepy eyes in humiliation
The kids tore into the pile of gifts, oohing and ahhing with elation
All were happy with the parents' participation
It was an exciting sensation, then finally' relaxation
And relief from that tantalizing occasion of expectation
And anticipation!

Grace Howard
Spokane, WA

Black Day

We all gather to mourn on this day
To shed precious tears from powerful, touched eyes
We sink low in our chairs
And listen to a trusted well-known voice who worships the good.

We think, why now?
How could this happen?
Why must we use these white tissues?
How can it be fair?

Looking around the room, no one is happy
No one is fighting back their emotions
Instead, I look forward and see the strong ones
And I start to remember all the amazing memories.

I think to myself, why so much black to a red heart full of love?
Then I suddenly remember how much I care
How much I love and miss the angel we lost
And so we all dread this sorrowful, black day.

Shainah Rugh
Punxsutawney, PA

A Goddess Who Lives at My House

I have a secret. . .
   There is a goddess who lives at my house
Stunning, dark and beautiful
   Black, olive eyes that dance with mirth
The sound of her laughter tickles my ears
   Her smile is like bright lights against a dark night
Compassion runs deep in her heart
   She masquerades as my daughter, turned eighteen
Hiding in human form, a princess
   Magical, mystical, stardust left in her wake
Truly, she is. . .
   A goddess who lives at my house

Kathleen Morreira
Lyons, OR

Reach for the Stars

Go for your dreams,
No matter how hard it may seem.
Keep going, for it may be rough,
But know inside that you are tough.
Never let go of that constant fight,
Even though it may take all your might.
Be yourself in all your actions—
That may someday lead you to satisfaction.
Your dreams are never that far,
If you just keep on reaching for the stars.

Rachel Salwey
Rushford, MN

Blue Barn

The belt, tight as a saddle cinch
Snaps from tractor to baler bin
Coughing green wedges onto the plains.

Hook in hand, I grab another.
I buck those bales upon the stack
That shoulders the blue barn wall.

Behind white paddock fences, bright
The quarter horses break their stare
To sniff alfalfa in the air—

Air heavy with the sifting dust.
For years, we work this way:
He hooks and rolls, I hook and stack.

The stenciled wicket, "Smokiam Ranch,"
White letters faded grey with wear—
Thirty head once, dwindled to two.

Refusing the help of most,
He stands in his tattered overalls,
Beyond the blue barn.

Sheryl Redding
Spokane, WA

Tortured Soul

I am a slave of my own soul.
It chains me to my grief
And tortures me with images of your death.
It shows me the tears in your eyes,
As they slowly cloud over.
It makes me feel the sweet caress of your lips on mine.
That kiss,
The kiss that came right before your demise,
Along with the taste that will not leave my mouth—
The taste of your blood as it flowed into your jowls.
It makes my hands itch at the feeling of the knife in my hand
And at the memory of the warmth of your dark, red elixir
Flowing into my palms.
But the most painful image of all
Is the smile on your face.
The smile that says "Thank you."
You dare to thank me for ending your immortal life?!
I may have helped you find peace, dear Huntress of the Night,
But whom I ask,
Who will help me find peace
When I am locked away in the dark,
Bloody memories that my soul torments me with?

Kimbra M. Warber
Gladstone, MO

It was in high school when I discovered my knack for writing. The poem "Tortured Soul" was inspired by an idea I had for a fiction novel (on which I am still working). Also included in this poem, along with several other original works, are my feelings: how I see life, how I see myself, and how I think others see me, as well as secret, dark thoughts that would otherwise grow stagnant and poisonous if unable to be expressed in a healthy manner. Poetry is my therapy, and it gets me through the darkest of times. Being able to write is my one, only, constant light in a world full of shadows.

Allah

Allah is great,
Allah is wise—
Allah knows truth from lies
and never, ever dies.
Allah, hold me,
mold me,
scold me,
heal me
and let me see
through Your eyes.
Allah, still my pride
and guide me to your prize. . .
and let me rise
from death to your skies.

Jim Rankin
San Diego, CA

For My Baby

Let me make a bridge for you
  so that you may have the
  ability to walk.

Let me make a sound for you,
  so that you may have the ability
  to talk

Let me live to encourage you
  so that you may have the
  ability to smile.

And let me only die for you
  so that you may truly
  live for awhile.

But first, let me share my thoughts
  with you
  to you, my mind I will give

So that you may have the
  yet unknown knowledge and
  yet unknown power to live

Carol Long
Merrill, WI

A Christmas Poem

On the Holy night of God's Son's birth,
A special star shined bright...
The Virgin who said "yes" to God
Held dear the events of that night.

The Son Who was born to save His people
Slept the entire night through;
Awakened only when visitors arrived,
He smiled and knew He would be true.

He knew His life was planned by God...
The Babe enjoyed the quietness of that night.
By performing miracles, preaching and healings in His life,
Knowing that suffering would be His plight.

But on that special night on earth,
He smiled to God above
For sending Him to do the job—
The job of preaching love.

Janie Zborowski
Washington, PA

Outside the Grasp

Like fish in a bowl
One-dimensional beings
Living in a state of odium
Accept obscure and cryptic clues
Which lead them to scary beliefs and doomsday anticipation
Seeking a familiar destiny
Yet, bord to kismet comfort
When nothing *big* happens
These anitquated thinkers tend to *make* it happen
Even to the destruction of others and self
The young
With visionary ideas, abilities and global exposure
Must be listened to, embraced, understood and loved
As they release us from a stalemate
And take us outside the grasp
To change!

Barbara Randall Clark
Orangeburg, SC

Born in Macon, GA, I am a retired educator/counselor/writer. My parents, sister, and two older brothers are deceased. One of my two living brothers is my twin. My spouse and I are parents to two adult children, Bobby and Angela. I have authored thirteen books and currently reside in Orangeburg, SC.

Untitled

I try to make my way in this world without you somehow
The void I feel from your loss is almost unbearable sometimes now
To never hear your voice or laughter, I feel so lost without you here
Going through each and every day—and still, I can't help but shed tears
In my heart now is where I will try to always keep you safe
That spot in my heart where no one can take your place
All I have are memories of you now to try to help me through every day
It's not the same as having you here
But I must deal with life, come what may
You are and always will be in my mind, heart and soul
There will always be some of those days
Where the pain of loss will take its toll
Death is never easy for ones to deal with who are left behind
We will remember you as the the loving, caring person you were
and the things that made you one-of-a-kind
Just remember, dear sister, how so very much you were loved
and now you are being kept safe by the good *Lord* above

Iesha Gentry
Smyrna, TN

What inspired this poem was the death of my beloved best friend, whom I have always called my sister. I met her when I was sixteen, and we were best friends/sisters for twenty years. The poem is about her and how I was feeling at the time of her death. This poem is in loving memory of Dena Hatfield-Henderson.

In Praise of Years

Fair you are, now that time
has tempered lines and looks
Full-bloom wears well and speaks
with no voice needed
The unkind cut that bled you
'til the flow subsided still
has left its brand. . .
a painful depth to gain
Now, upright again,
vision cleared
You lost...but yet
you gained, for your scope
of giving has grown
and softened
With patient ways, you'll
give again, in fullness
never imagined. . .
with feelings
never
known

Richard Laulainen Wagner
La Jolla, CA

Temptation

Out in the open
stood a closed door.
A man gazed upon it
as it beckoned for more.

He would not open it
and was certain of that—
it was curiosity
that did in the cat.

But when he went home
and attempted to sleep,
that door haunted him;
in his dreams, it seeped.

So the very next day,
he twisted the knob...
darkness pulled him in,
and his life it did rob.

A second chance was not given,
and the man was no more.
For sometimes, it is better
to ignore a closed door.

Cass Brandenstein
McDonald, PA

A Tapestry of Memories

When old friends reunite with soul mates of years past,
Time has come to reminisce of events their hearts have long held fast.

There are treasured memories of the past, which are recalled with ease;
Others must be mended—from bits and pieces of tattered memories.

Once those reassembled fragments allow thoughts to regress;
They have rewoven memories into a tapestry of happiness.

Friendships that remain after many years have passed by
Provide the twine that bind memories of which we now rely.

Doyle Pugh
Independence, MO

I was born October 10, 1935 in Moberly, MO, then grew up near Versailles, MO at the northern edge of the beautiful Ozark Hills. Several of my ancestors were poets; however, I was in my late sixties before I started writing poetry. I have one book published, View from the Side Roads, *but this is the first poem I have submitted to a contest. Though limited vision has restricted my physical sight, through poetry I wish to share my vision of life in a positive light.*

Red-Winged Angel

Her wings are stained
a crimson red
by things done, too horrible
to be said
Her body aches from carrying the
weight of her heart
and every day, it threatens to
tear her apart
Her head hangs down in
shame and regret
but she has always known
her path is set
She does her job without a fuss
she has no choice
and she never complains
She has no voice
She cannot ever cry, for
she has no tears
but her sorrow only grows
through the years
As you sit and pray in the
broken cathedral
I bet you have never once thought
of the red-winged angel

Victoria Furtado
Woodland, CA

Growing Old Is Not a Curse

Our birthdays give us reason
to throw a party every year,
Invite our close friends over
for cake and cookies and beer.

Let us not confuse that day
by thinking it means we're growing up;
Growing older can be an exciting trip
If you remember, "It's okay to be a pup."

Over the years you may discover
there's a lesson we must find;
It's not getting older that's the issue,
growing up is just a state of mind.

You'll see this trait in men, it's true;
when they age, some don't mature.
What no one tells you, it's their choice—
staying young is just their nature!

So while birthdays may be piling up
"Growing up" may not be your fate.
You have the option—yes, it is your choice—
to remain a kid at heart till eighty-eight.

Ken Foote
Grand Haven, MI

Progression by Digression

There will come a time when I will have been scheduled
an appointment, and death has become my fate;
Reminders by phone, a letter in the mail are now obsolete.
Better yet, I will be kneeling, soon revealing
the worthiness of myself when it's time to speak,
As I lay my life and soul on the ground,
displayed at my Rescuer's feet.
When I open my mouth and the words come out,
the minimizations of my thoughts are discrete.
Although desolate, I will not retreat—
instead, face the storm with honesty,
Knowing the best policy is to diminish the falsity
behind the feeling of being weak,
To understand not on your knees...
instead, shameless on your feet.
But before I could see, I believed I only needed me
and the rupturing acts for immediate relief;
Now, my overall relief is obtained through belief
and the fact He is permitting me to see.
Throughout the storm, His love endures,
which leads me right back to His feet—
Not grasping that from the beginning,
this was the goal I was seeking to achieve.

Donald Steven Gray
Mount Juliet, TN

Golden Pathway

Here we are folks, we've
　　reached the Golden Age.
Don't engage in rage—just
　　happily turn the page.
Enjoy your family and friends,
　　good times always near;
encapture the rapture
　　without any fear.
Turn your eyes to the heavenly
　　blue skies above.
We're still here, my dears, so
　　embrace the circle of love.

Sing and dance, travel the
　　beautiful majestic world;
Read good books, take tender
　　care of your health.
Keep smiling, stay in touch with
　　your insight unfurled.
It's all yours—your passion of
　　living, your wealth!

Nedra S. Moe
Winston, OR

If Christmas Hadn't Happened

What if Christmas hadn't happened, if Jesus hadn't been born as a baby?
Our salvation would not be certain, it would only be a maybe.
Salvation would depend on works and the good that we do—
Could we measure up for a lifetime, or only an hour or two?
If Christmas hadn't happened, the Bible would be untrue;
It would only be a fairytale, a myth for me and you.
The prophets would only be novelists writing stories of a king,
There would be no star of Bethlehem, no carols would we sing.
If Christmas hadn't happened, we would never know our God,
For He would not have walked with us upon this earthly sod.
We would have no intercessor between us and God's ears,
So our prayers would go unanswered, we'd be alone with our fears.
If Christmas hadn't happened, our sins would not be forgiven;
For without the shedding of Jesus' blood, we cannot enter Heaven.
There would be no hope for any of us, the devil would have his say.
If Christmas hadn't happened, we have no Light, no Truth, no Way.
But thank God, Christmas did happen—God sent forth His Son to earth.
So we have the prophets stories, we have the virgin birth.
Jesus did come as a tiny baby; He was tempted as you and I.
Without sin, He willingly went to the cross, shed His blood and died.
He rose again on Easter morn, He saved us from our sin...
His grace is all-sufficient, if we only let Him in.

Lavena I. Toon
Ponca City, OK

Begging You, Please

Tattered and torn, broken, black and blue
This guardian angel, sent for you
Beautiful and strong before
But your journey broke him
Made him sore
Trying to protect you
Himself he threw
Onto the wreckage that was cast upon you
At times, your journey was an abomination
Your angel tried to guide you to Salvation
This painful journey
How much can he take
The dangers, the damage
There's no mistake
His body weighs heavy
His heart still aches
Breathing and sighing
He's brought to his knees
Softly, he's crying begging you, please
For my life, I give
Do not forsake
You are a beautiful creation
Not a mistake

Cassandra Woods
Valley Center, GA

In My Lifetime

Resume

Staggered stands for returned parcels
Delivered unintentionally
For the moon hinders its fall
Into the bright star
Inevitable
Fatigue spills red
Like tears behind gloss glass
When the end is nigh
All intentions are no longer taxable
A mended mind is one at fault
The guilt, hidden
Locked like a vault
Sought by distraught
More ink will be spilled
All that they've fought
But nothing fulfilled
When doves part their ways
A relaxed tension, let build
If distance is fear
And they, often near
Perhaps the return
Was below their yield
Above tended grass field
Like stitches in the atmosphere
Much knowledge arises
Quick to the ear

Joshua J. Gutierrez
Santa Clara, CA

A Grandmother's Blessing

Wishing you a stack of warm chocolate chip cookies
On a red plate that says, "You're Special, We Love You"
Served with a tall glass of cold milk and coffee, too,
On a tray with a flag flying red, white and blue.
A book with a story with your favorite characters,
A new puppy with ears that are velvety soft—
Snuggling close and inviting you to rest
On pillows that are stacked like a cloud on a loft.
And memories that are sweet and fun to remember
Of your special talents and good dreams that came true,
And your Heavenly Father saying, "You are the one."
Reminding your spirit of incredible you.
Sending words that encourage, like *faith, hope* and *love*,
And a touch to your ears so they hear loud and clear.
Feel the guardian angels that stay day and night
So that you ponder that Jesus is standing so near.
Have a hug and a high-five—a pat on the back.
Put your dancing shoes on, take a spin on the floor;
Sing a song with the Holy Spirit about gladness.
Expect goodness and kindness and blessings galore.
Love, Emma—AKA Grandma

Mary Durkin Tremblay
Napa, CA

My way to honor God and encourage others is by using words He gives me. The first time a child said, "You are just like a grandma," I was twenty years old. I've worked with children all my life, and these words were repeated so many times I couldn't help smiling. One day I heard the Lord say, "You have a grandmother's anointing." No one is too young or too old to give unconditional love to. I wish happiness to others; that's my "Grandmother's Blessing."

Six Degrees of Separation

They say everything happens for a reason in time
measuring where we are by latitude
and longitude of the sky's lines
that there's six degrees of separation to life, but why?

Separating past six degrees, leaving my future somewhat foreseen. . .
a bloodline of the da Vinci gene: mind over matter
my heart is the one who leads
I'm so close to you
but far from six degrees

My path took a detour to see evil's face
six degrees of separation is another secret place.

When I look at you
I see the smile has left your eyes
Rolling sadness of our world's demise
a generation that's deaf to love's unknown cry. . .

'Cause without love
six degrees of separation eventually comes to die. . .
The realms bleed together, forming hallucinogenic states of mind
where realities uncover truths of dreams with an absence of time
Separating each being in realms we cannot come to find

Six degrees of separation
a theory so questioned, with no answer before we die. . .

Six degrees of separation is
unattainable when high. . .
and pausing what we consider
the measurement of time

Marlaina Robinson
South Lake Tahoe, CA

Aunt Julia

She was the last
  Of the line
Which was
  All very fine

So I thought
  She would know
All the
  Family history

So I quizzed about
  Uncles and aunts
  and family transplants

She said, "If anyone asks
  You can plainly see
You can't get it from me
  I don't live
    in the *past*

Graham Bell Conner
New Market, VA

The Fairytale I Thought You Were

Once upon a time, I thought you
Were my Prince Charming,
You were the King of hearts.

But you turned out to be a joker
In my deck of cards.
You brought down the queen,
Because you thought you were an ace.

You let the rain fall, you figured
You were a diamond.
Everyone around you,
You pictured as a peasant.

I thought you were my
Once upon a time
But the story ended fairly quick
As we bid adieu and lived—
sadly, never after—
In our once upon a time.

Samantha Glisson
Spokane, WA

Reminiscence

Every Friday night when I was small,
Mom would bring in the washtub from out in the hall,
heat tons of water in the old cook pot
and scrub us while it was nice and hot.

We didn't have bathrooms or electric lights
and went to bed with the chickens most every night.
Except on Saturday, we would go into town—
have an ice cream cone, or just walk around.

Sometimes, Mom would play bingo at the fire hall
or browse through the dry goods to find a doll.
If it was near Christmas, there would be lots of singing;
and, of course, on the corner, bells would be ringing.

In summer, the old folks would sit on the Courthouse lawn
and reminisce about when they were young.
A bunch of us kids would sit there in awe
and hear incredible stories that they'd tell us all.

Sometimes I think about those years,
when I was young and had no fears—
When life was so simple and down-to-earth.
I just wasn't aware of what they were worth.

Today with our modern technology,
most of us have lost the ability
to look back and see how it used to be. . .
when life was so simple and fancy-free.

Lottie L. Smith
New Columbia, PA

The Loss of Innocence

Maybe it begins when we find out the truth about Santa,
or perhaps it begins after our first kiss. . .

When puberty hits, or when simple matters blow up
into heart-crushing experiences.

It's a weird thing,
almost inhumane, really.

As if in order to grow up, in order to become who we want to be,
we have to stop being naïve.

We have to face the world, one struggle at a time,
and face it with bravery.

Bravery and strength,
whatever that is—good luck finding it at age thirteen, or even eighteen.

Because ignorance is not always bliss,
and arrogance gains nothing.

To lose innocence
is to face reality.

It is to gain the maturity every human needs.
Because in order to become that person that your eight-year-old self
imagined you'd be,

you have to realize that life's not easy;
you have to shed the childlike ways.

Perhaps the loss of innocence isn't as bad as it seems.
If it wasn't for this pivotal moment,

well then, I suppose we wouldn't know
what love actually means.

Holly Gambrell
Union Bridge, MD

Ageless: An Ode to the Older Generation

With tall tales and big fish stories,
Knowledge of many years gone by,
Such a long life and loved ones lost. . .
So many tears shed.
With wrinkles and lines on your face,
Each one marks an event in life.
Faded eyes that have seen a lifetime,
But are still filled with love and wisdom,
Bones that creak with each move,
Backs that ache and knees that smart,
Arms that open eagerly for hugs
From children, grandchildren and loved ones.
Now getting around in wheelchairs or with canes and walkers,
Being cared for in "homes" by affectionate staff members—
Sharing with them your affection and laughter,
With a secret yearning to be younger again.
In truth, you may not be in your prime,
Yet you are far from ancient; still, you are a treasure to behold.
Our older generation, what they are is ageless—
Never to be forgotten, but cherished for the treasure they are.
Why?
For their intellect beyond bound,
Their advice should be taken to heart;
Because they lived the history taught to today's younger population,
This era is truly wise and ageless.

Kellie Frey
Saint Marys, PA

Gardens

My eyes have witnessed God's wondrous gifts as my life unfolded
and was blessed every day to behold all that His hands molded.
From atop the majestic mountains, as far as my eyes could see,
was God's breathtaking masterpiece that lay before me.
Walking through the meadows, I've smelled the beautiful flowers
as they opened their petals to the spring showers.
In the forest I've been awed by the birds' symphonies. . .
as their glorious songs flowed through the trees.
I've tasted the bitter, savored the sweet,
felt the oceans waves splash upon my feet.
God's love for us is His greatest gift to give,
in creating this beautiful world for us to live.
In His earthly gardens, God walked by my side;
in His heavenly gardens, I shall forever abide.

Larry Dalrymple
Effingham, SC

Sandy

Sandy blew onto the shore,
She kicked the sand up from the beach;
Her sand filled the basements.
The wind trimmed the trees—
Power lines were dashed to the ground.
Subways were useless,
Elevators came to a standstill.
Cars floated away, as if on a river.
Who can assess all this horrible loss?
Some lives were snuffed out, others insist on being born. . .
Some lives remain, others are gone.

Margaret SanGregory
Bellevue, OH

Untitled

You kept me around,
standing your ground,
waiting by my grave. . .
watching me die before your eyes,
this is the game you wanted to play.
Winning was the only way—you stayed
until the end, when I was lowered into my grave.

Heidi Christine Jones
Monterey, CA

Ignis Fatuus

Some say that a foolish heart of light
Will miss four hundred years of spite.
And a benevolent spirit will not cease to ignite
Any rock that would put up a fight.

How unfortunate that the tides of time
Have allowed mans' mind to turn to swine.
And in the blinding light of holy day,
They rot...and shovel their mouths full of hay.

They said that her head was not like the rest
So they cursed and shoved her out of their nest.
The days grew short, and the nights grew long
And the only salvation was that of your song.

Within the times of ache and illness,
I heard the whispers of wind's unending stillness.
And to save a life that has grown dead
Is to swim in the sea of Black and Red.

Some know the pride and beauty of her breed
Is the perfect recipe for what they need.
And the timely coming of a great wit
Will keep the darkest candle forever lit.

What was said before will always be said after,
And to survive is to hunt for its laughter.
Behold, the next muse to aid the force,
And speak a story that will guide the horse.

Angela Perna
San Diego, CA

The Alabama Farm

The farm is the place in the world where I feel most at home,
a place of red clay, green grass, and lush trees.

The farm is where my precious, furry friends lay—
my Scout, my Bo, my Candy, Margo, Sam, and Teebo.

It is the first place I see when I know I am home
and the last place I see when I must go.

I can be there for a short time or long,
but it lasts until I am there again.

It is always there and always will be. . .
it is there that I know I will once again be.

It is the place where I am most comfortable,
it is in my heart and my mind.

It is the place that gives me the warmest memories. . .
home, the Alabama farm.

Jessica Birchfield Quisenberry
Lexington, VA

In My Next Fifty Years

In my next fifty years, they'll be no sorrow or pain—
Just love in my heart, and dances in the rain.
They'll be time to savor all my wishes and my dreams,
Time to be thankful for life and what it means.

Just to sit and marvel at grandkids when they play,
To be at peace with the world—"finally," someday.
Just to look forward to all the sunny skies. . .
On my next fifty years, no more tears in my eyes.

I've been a daughter, sister, a mother and a wife.
In my next fifty years, I'm going to love my life!
I have made mistakes and lost loves along the way;
To my next fifty years, my faith will always stay.

I will know love, and be loved, and to myself be true.
In my next fifty years, I will spend them all with you.
You came into my life when I had lost my way—
You gave me the strength to love again someday.

In my next fifty years, what a trip it's gonna be!
I'm so glad I found you to come along with me.

Judy R. Smith
Afton, TN

Guardian Angel

A hundred voices shifting in a crowd
Speak words that buzz like broken TV screens
And punctuate the air with jagged beams;
Ideas that never mattered ring too loud.
While stony feet traverse on tired threads
And slamming doors are felt from floors beneath—
As though the ground were gnashing at its teeth—
The silent bird is filled with nameless dread.
I fear the static wears upon your ears,
For you keep losing track of measured sand
Because you cannot see the Keeper's hand
And always dash the glass walls of your fears.
I know you've seen the Gardener's work in bloom
But will you trust in seeds beneath the ice
Though seasons without spring have marked you twice
And earth may seem like nothing but a tomb?
True, the world is cluttered with surprise;
Amid kaleidoscopes of shifting things,
The future's held by watchful diamond eyes.
Can you hear the brush of holy wings?

Hailey Trier
Middleton, WI

The Showman

He brightened your life
from the moment you met him.

Although he is gone,
we will never forget him.

A giant of a man,
in heart and in stature...

Just knowing he liked you
brought you a feeling of rapture.

He touched all our lives—
mine, regrettably, for only a short while.

Remember all the stories he told,
in his own unique style?

He knew thousands of people:
aided presidents, made movies, too.

We will remember all of these tales,
and we will smile when we do.

Perhaps he was testing us,
perhaps he believed them to be true.

Whatever the reason he told them. . .

Showman, we are far better persons
for having known you.

Lorna Willhelm
Waco, TX

Afraid

Why was I afraid to speak to you
When my words could have calmed your heart?
Why was I afraid to touch you
When my warmth could have caressed your soul?
Why was I afraid to express my love for you
When my heart and soul were overflowing with it?
Looking back, I am afraid I let you down—
Now, I am afraid because I have lost you.

Brenda Galeles
Wisconsin Rapids, WI

My sister Ann passed away in 2011. This poem expresses the regrets that I have since she exited my life. Becoming separated from someone when you were inseparable for so many years is extremely hard. If only I could go back in time and have one more conversation with her. I miss her encouraging words, her jokes, her opinions, just the sound of her voice. Hopefully by releasing my emotions through writing, other readers will be able to relate. And since Ann was a lover of poetry, I feel there is no better way to do it.

Teachers

I know, teachers are just angels in disguise—
They're loving, patient, and exceptionally wise.

They are our children's mothers and fathers,
when we can't be there during the day.

They're safe under their wings—
Then at three, sent our way.

hey not only teach them math, language, and reading,
They teach them how to succeed in life and keep on succeeding.

It takes an angel to teach your child and mine,
And if you look real close, you'll see their wings from behind.

Tammie Farrow
Benton, AR

Leaves

From the wind, the breeze will blow,
swaying the trees to and fro.

Sending the leaves to the ground,
as the light hits them to the earth. . .

As they blow away from here to make a new home,
where they may lay on the ground once more.

Pam Brittain
La Junta, CO

Story Where You Least Expect It

I've found a book
in the middle of the ocean
It keeps me up at night
and drowns me in my sleep
Taking apart my lungs
and reconstructing it
with the plot
and the meaning

Faith Ginter
Winnipeg, MB

Dreams

Dreams can be almost anything:
A flying pig, or a squirrel that sings.
Dreams can be in any place...
They can be in outer space.

In the sky or on the ground,
Killer whale spinning 'round and 'round.
Counting sheep: one, two, three.
I'm trying to sleep, don't bother me.

Jessica Sidney Stark
Seminole, FL

A Day Without Love

A dream is all I've ever had
to find a love of my own
I have never found someone
whose heart beats my same tone
I need to know that I am loved
and my heart will never be broken
I want someone to hold me tight
and listen to the words I've spoken
I have been happy and gave it many tries
but all that has been shattered with heartbreak and all lies

Alisha Gale Streetman
Ravenswood, WV

Storm

The above screams.
The under churns at our beat.
In the blackness, we stop at one of the flows,
where the gray one drinks—long and unhurried—
As the tall ones,
In their browns and greens,
Bend
And buck
Under the falls.

Thomas Lepore
Simi Valley, CA

Thomas (Tommy) Lepore is a senior at Chapman University, who plans to attend graduate school next year. A lover of books and writing from a young age, he aspires to become an English professor and write during the summer and holidays. Outside of poetry like "Storm," Tommy enjoys reading and writing fiction—specifically fantasy fiction, like The Chronicles of Narnia, Lord of the Rings *and the* Song of Ice and Fire. *He is currently revising his novel, which he hopes to get published one day.*

A Soldier's Inspiration

One day soon, things will turn around,
And shortly after, we'll all be homeward bound.
No more fighting; no more tears—
For we have faced our greatest fears.

We'll march home with our heads held high,
in honor of those who didn't have to die.
They gave us courage, they gave us reason;
They fought for us against the treason.

In their names, we continue the fight—
only to up hold what we know is right.

Tabitha G. Smith
Greenville, TX

*This is dedicated to my family and fellow service members and inspired by
my grandmother, who wrote a similar poem when my dad left for boot camp.
Raised in the military and then serving as a marine myself, I see all the things
most don't seem to understand, yet take it for granted. This is to remind us
all that those in the military feel like many of us and give their all—by choice,
to protect us and what we have. Thank the Lord for the freedoms we have
and the gift of choice and sacrifice. Semper Fi (Always Faithful)!*

I Will Stand

Most of what I called "mine" is gone now
My face is gone and replaced with steel
My hands have left, and hooks took up residence
The feet I called my own have taken more steps than I
Legs seemed to have kicked the bucket
Spring-loaded pegs seem to be getting me everywhere now
It might be hard for you to see me smile
My dance might get you to smile
Getting from place to place to harder than I remember
And yet I still stand and fight the pain back for the National Anthem
The tears you see are not from pain but from pride for my country
I still salute the red, white and blue with no hands
Not for the ones who don't, but for the ones who no longer can

Wolf Ponton
Stagecoach, NV

The Common Man

As I look back at the long, gray shadows of my life
and I feel the cold wind against my face,
I wonder if I'll ever travel the journeys of my dreams
and hold the treasures of my life in my hands.

But as I remember her soft cheek against mine
and the tiny hands of children in mine,
I realize I have travelled the journeys of my dreams
and held the treasures of my life in my hands.

Gene Fritz
Gypsum, KS

Love Is a Wonderful Passion

Love is a wonderful passion
The burning sensation makes the strongest heart smirk
Butterflies begin to overwhelm your body
Your finger tips start to tremble
Heart beats fast, and your eyes shut
Lips touch, and your body gets warm all over
You pull away and bite your lip
You hug and wish that it had never ended
Love is a wonderful passion

Katelynn Cherrie McKinney
Omaha, NE

Honor and Rats

You might have riches, you might have fame
You might have home, and plenty of gain
You might have this, you might have that
But I have honor—you, a rat

You might have fine clothes, you might have lands
You might have good food, and no demands
You might have this, you might have that
But I have honor—you, a rat

You might have a crown, you might have swords
You might have heirs, and you might have lords
You might have this, you might have that
But I have honor—you, a rat

Abigail Grace Harris
Mountain Grove, MO

Little Beach

Here there are dreams that linger in whirlwinds,
rising up to the heavens,
whisking the sands below, trodden by the feet of innocence.
And whence we return after an age passed,
still we find the child among the sand and sea grass.

George Charles Millak
Tigrad, OR

This poem was inspired by my grandparents who lived on the Oregon Coast for more than thirty years in a little town called Gearheart. My siblings and I spent much of our youth there, trifling about the seascape, building castles, and catching clams before the briny breakers.

Walking with a Memory

The angels came one month ago
and took my love from me.
The garden walks, the loving talks
are now just a memory.
My loss I know is Heaven's gain,
but your spirit with me still remains.
Your gentle voice calls out to me
from somewhere up above.
"Come, sweetheart, lets take that walk—
for you are still my only love."

James Harwood
Spencer, WI

To me, poetry has always been a way to cope with life's eternal ebbs and flows, its tragedies and its joys. This particular poem was written a month after I lost my love of fourteen years to cancer. In loving memory of Judith Omelian: December 22, 1949–November 2, 2012.

Spring

Spring, it's when the cold turns to warm
It's when the flowers bloom
a rainbow of colors
and the sky is as blue as the ocean
it's when a soft cool breeze blows
through your hair
you roll down a fuzzy, green hill as the sun
shines upon your face
but what I love most about spring is
the birds sing a song so sweet

Jade Bateman
Dubois, IN

Only but a Dream

Have you ever heard a whippoorwill
singing in the night?
Have you ever saw a shooting star
while it was in flight?
Have you ever saw in the fall
the changing of the leaves,
or maybe felt a cool summer breeze
blowing softly through the trees?
How peaceful and pleasant all these
worldly things must surely seem—
but when God comes to carry us home,
it was only but a dream.

Ronald Kent Collins
Jesup, GA

No Longer Alone

I sit alone,
With tons of people around me.

I am alone.
But then, I look up
And see your smiling face.
You extend your hand to me,
And I take it.

I rise up with you,
And I stand, holding your hand,
Right beside you.

I am alone
No longer.

Victoria A. Dominguez
Sonora, CA

Over the Rainbow

That place over the rainbow's really there—
God made it for all of us to forever share.
That place over the rainbow where we'll go
Is lovelier than anything you and I now know.
Delightful dancing on the clouds is His most sparkling, bright tomorrow,
And flying with the angels, where there's only joy and never sorrow.
That place over the rainbow, where we'll see
Extra-extra beautiful, that it will always be. . .
And extra-extra beautiful, the Lord's love always is for you and me.

Anthony J. Golden
Chula Vista, CA

The first lines of "Over the Rainbow" came to me easily. A beautiful inspiration from two wonderful ladies (namely, a mother and daughter) helped with finishing this poem.

Finding a Snowflake

It's a snowy day in February, and I'm thinking of you—
not the bills on the dirty counter, all past-due.
Each snowflake that's falling is a piece of my heart,
torn in the rejecting wind. .drifting apart.
It carries me from dusk till dawn;
but don't worry, Daddy, soon enough, I'll be gone.
If you ever wish to see me, you better hurry fast;
run to catch me, before I've passed.
If you try really hard, you can find me where I used to play
In that strong oak tree. Now, listen to what I say. . .
If you want to hear my cry, and *if* you care to find,
listen to your heart, and open up your mind.

Tanna Coalson
Hico, TX

Index of Poets

CPSIA information can be obtained at www.ICGtesting.com
Printed in the USA
BVOW070426020513

319660BV00001B/3/P